BREAKING THE CODE

Also by Hugh Whitemore

Stevie
Pack of Lies

HUGH WHITEMORE

BREAKING THE CODE

Based on the book 'Alan Turing, The Enigma' by Andrew Hodges

AMBER LANE PRESS

All rights whatsoever in this play are strictly reserved and application for performance, etc. should be made before rehearsal to:
Judy Daish Associates Ltd.
83 Eastbourne Mews
London W2 6LQ
No performance may be given unless a licence has been obtained.

First published in 1987 by
Amber Lane Press Ltd.
9 Middle Way
Oxford OX2 7LH

Typeset by Oxford Computer Typesetting

Printed and manufactured in Great Britain by
Cotswold Press Ltd., Oxford

ISBN: 0 906399 80 7

Breaking the Code was first presented by Michael Redington in association with Duncan C. Weldon and Jerome Minskoff at the Yvonne Arnaud Theatre, Guildford on 15th September, 1986, and subsequently at the Theatre Royal, Haymarket, London on 21st October, 1986, with the following cast:

ALAN TURING:	Derek Jacobi
MICK ROSS:	Dave Hill
CHRISTOPHER MORCOM:	Richard Stirling
SARA TURING:	Isabel Dean
RON MILLER:	Paul Slack
JOHN SMITH:	Michael Malnick
DILLWYN KNOX:	Michael Gough
PAT GREEN:	Joanna David
NIKOS:	Dean Winters

Director: Clifford Williams
Designer: Liz da Costa
Lighting Designer: Mick Hughes

For Clifford

CHARACTERS
in order of appearance

MICK ROSS
ALAN TURING
CHRISTOPHER MORCOM
SARA TURING
RON MILLER
JOHN SMITH
DILLWYN KNOX
PAT GREEN
NIKOS

ACT ONE

SCENE ONE

ALAN TURING *enters with* MICK ROSS.

TURING *is about 40: untidily dressed, unkempt appearance, an occasional stammer.* ROSS *is carrying a file of papers; he is a Detective Sergeant.*

ROSS: Sorry to keep you waiting, sir. Sit down.
        [TURING *sits;* ROSS *sits facing him.*]
        Make yourself comfortable. [*opens the file*] Well now, let's get the basic facts sorted out. We're talking about a burglary that occurred on January the twenty-third, and you are Mr Spurling.

TURING: No — Turing.

ROSS: I beg your pardon?

TURING: My name is Turing, not Spurling.

ROSS: Sorry, sir, beg your pardon. Bloody illiterate, some of our young police constables. [*displays a sheet of paper*] Just look at this atrocious writing. It could be Spurling, Spilling . . . Tilling.

TURING: Well, it's T-t-turing. [*spelling*] T-u-r-i-n-g.

ROSS: [*writing*] Alan Mathison Turing. Is that right?

TURING: Yes.

ROSS: Right. Mick Ross. Detective Sergeant.

TURING: How do you do.

ROSS: How do you do, sir. [*looks at the file of papers*] You live at Hollymeade, Adlington Road, Wilmslow?

TURING: Yes.

ROSS: And you work at Manchester University?

TURING: Yes.

ROSS: So it's Professor Turing?

TURING: Mr Turing is p-p-perfectly adequate.

ROSS: Right. [*glances at* TURING] Not a native north-countryman?

TURING: No.

ROSS: No, I thought not. How long have you been here?

TURING: Four years; since 1948.

ROSS: [*as he writes*] It's an unusual name, Turing. Don't think I've come across it before.

TURING: Scottish.

ROSS: Ah. Whereabouts?

TURING: I'm sorry . . . ?

ROSS: Whereabouts in Scotland do you come from?

TURING: No, I, um — the Turings are of Scottish descent —

ROSS: Oh, I see.

TURING: — they came to England some time ago.

ROSS: Before you were born?

TURING: In the seventeenth century, I think.

ROSS: Ah — right. [*a grin; then looks at the file*] Now, sir, this burglary . . . can you tell me exactly what happened?

TURING: Well, as I explained to the police constable, I got back home on Wednesday evening and found that the house had been b-b-broken into.
       [*Pause.*]

ROSS: Yes . . . ?

TURING: I telephoned the police and then I made a list of what was missing — of what seemed to be missing.

ROSS: [*showing a sheet of paper to* TURING] Is this your list?

TURING: Yes.

ROSS: A shirt, five fish knives, a pair of tweed trousers, three pairs of shoes, a compass, an electric shaver, and a half empty bottle of sherry. Not much of a haul.

TURING: No, I don't, uh . . .
       [*Brief pause.*]

ROSS: Yes, sir?

TURING: I live very simply. Possessions, *per se,* mean very little to me.

ROSS: Possessions what, sir?

TURING: What?

ROSS: I didn't hear what you said.

TURING: Possessions *per se*: for their own sake.

ROSS: Ah yes. [*refers to the report*] Now you said — you said to the police constable — you told him that you had some idea who might've committed the crime. Is that so?

TURING: Well, yes.
       [*Brief pause.* ROSS *waits.*]
       I think his name's George.

ROSS: George . . . ?

TURING: Yes.

ROSS: George what?

TURING: I don't know.

ROSS: Who is this man? Do you know him?

TURING: No.

ROSS: Can you describe him?

TURING: No, I've never seen him.

ROSS: But you know his name?

TURING: Well yes, somebody told me.

ROSS: Told you what, sir?

TURING: That this man George might be a burglar.

ROSS: Who told you?

TURING: Well, um — a young man came to the door. He was selling something. Brushes or something. He told me to be careful because, uh . . . he'd heard somebody talking about a b-b-burglary. They were planning a burglary, you see. He overheard them.

ROSS: [*eyebrows raised*] He heard this man George making some sort of a plan to burgle your house?

TURING: Not my house specifically, no. A house in my neighbourhood. Or so I gather. That's what I was told. [*brief pause*] This young man — the brush salesman — he said he knew the person who was t-t-talking. George. He recognised him, do you see? [*brief pause*] And, um . . . well, that's all, really.

ROSS: Where did this conversation take place?

TURING: What conversation?

ROSS: The conversation this young man overheard.

TURING: In a pub, I think.

ROSS: In a pub?

TURING: I think so, yes.

[*Pause.*]

ROSS: I'm puzzled, Mr Turing. How did the subject come up? Why did this brush salesman decide to tell you about a conversation he'd overheard in a pub?

TURING: Well, I suppose . . . to warn me, I suppose.

ROSS: It's very curious, don't you think? It's an odd thing to have happened.

TURING: Is it?

ROSS: I'd have thought so. [*brief pause*] Why didn't you inform the police at the time?

TURING: It never occurred to me to do so. [*brief pause*] I mean, it was only a casual remark. He just said be careful, keep your eyes open. I didn't pay much attention, really.

ROSS: Mmm. [*a moment of reflection*] When did he come to your house?

TURING: Three or four weeks ago.

ROSS: Who did he work for, do you remember? What sort of brushes was he selling?

TURING: I've no idea. It may not have been brushes. I forget.

ROSS: It'd be useful if you could remember.

TURING: Yes, I'll try.

ROSS: Please do.

> *[The telephone rings.]*
>
> Excuse me, sir. *[lifts the receiver]* Hello, Ross. Yes . . . ? When . . . ? Right. *[replaces the receiver; picks up the file]* Sorry, sir — bit of a problem. *[rises to his feet]* We'll be in touch, okay? One of the lads will show you out.
>
> *[ROSS exits.]*

> *[Lighting change: summer afternoon.]*

SCENE TWO

> CHRISTOPHER MORCOM *enters, wearing school uniform. He is about 17.*

CHRIS: He should never have lied; that was the real mistake. I have some very definite ideas of right and wrong, and it's always wrong to lie.

TURING: Perhaps he was afraid.

CHRIS: Of course he was afraid. He'd cribbed during the Latin exam; he knew he'd be found out, he knew he'd be punished. But lying made everything a hundred times worse.

> *[SARA's voice is heard.]*

SARA: *[off]* Alan! Alan!

TURING: Oh, Lord — that's my mother.

> *[SARA enters; she wears clothes appropriate for the late 1920s.]*

SARA: Ah, here you are. Do forgive me. I thought I heard the doorbell, but I wasn't quite sure, I was out in the garden, you see. Do forgive me.

> *[There is a brief, rather awkward, silence.]*
>
> Alan dear, won't you introduce your friend?

TURING: *[gracelessly]* Oh, sorry — this is Christopher Morcom.

SARA: How do you do, Christopher.

CHRIS: How do you do, Mrs Turing.

SARA: I'm delighted to meet you at long last. Alan has talked so

much about you, and I kept saying to him, 'Do invite
Christopher down for a weekend' — never expecting for a
moment that he would. No matter what we say, he always
endeavours to keep his school friends to himself. I think
perhaps he's ashamed of us.
[TURING *squirms;* CHRIS *responds with a shy smile.*]
Did you have a comfortable journey?

CHRIS: Yes, thank you. I got the one-forty-five. First stop Guildford.

SARA: Oh good. [*smiles at him*] Do sit down, won't you? Sit over
here, by me.

CHRIS: Thank you.
[SARA *and* CHRIS *sit by the table.*]

SARA: Alan tells me that your family has a flat in town.

CHRIS: Well, it's only very small. Near Victoria Station, actually.
My mother uses it as a studio.

SARA: A studio . . . ?

CHRIS: For her sculpture. She makes sculptures and so on.

SARA: How exciting.

CHRIS: Well, not really.

SARA: Isn't it? I would've thought it would be rather exciting to
have a mother who is an artist.

CHRIS: It's only a hobby, really. She spends most of her time
looking after the goats.

SARA: What goats?

CHRIS: We have a goat farm at home.

SARA: Near Victoria Station?

CHRIS: No, Bromsgrove. Our real home is in Bromsgrove.

SARA: Oh, I see.

CHRIS: Bromsgrove is in Worcestershire.

SARA: Yes, I love Worcestershire: the garden of England.

TURING: That's Kent, mother.

SARA: [*ignoring this*] I often wish we'd been able to spend more
time in this country, but of course that wasn't possible.
Has Alan told you about our travels?

CHRIS: No.

SARA: Ah, well — my husband was in the Indian Civil Service.
He's retired now. Ill health. But for years we roamed
around India: Bezwada, Madras, Kurnool, Chatrapur.
Alan was very nearly born in Chatrapur.

TURING: How can you be nearly born somewhere? It doesn't make
sense.

SARA: [*irritated*] Oh, Alan — please.

TURING: Look at it logically.

SARA: I do wish you wouldn't say things like that.

TURING: Like what?

SARA: You know how it annoys me. [*to* CHRIS] Alan has such an unruly streak in his nature. I'm sure you're much more level-headed.

CHRIS: Well, I . . .

SARA: [*not waiting*] Anyway, I'm glad that you've become such firm friends. Without a steadying influence it's all too easy for a clever boy to grow into a mere intellectual crank.

TURING: [*tartly*] Thank you, mother.

SARA: I don't mean that unkindly; it's a very real danger. [*to* CHRIS] How long have you been at Sherborne?

CHRIS: A year longer than Turing. [*correcting himself*] Alan.

SARA: And are you enjoying it?

CHRIS: Very much.

SARA: Alan's brother went to Marlborough and did quite well there; but I was afraid it might be a little rigid for someone like Alan. Choosing the right school is so tremendously important, don't you think? — and I'm very impressed with Sherborne.

TURING: It's not that wonderful.

SARA: Of course it is. [*glancing sharply*] What's wrong with it?

TURING: Well, for one thing, they don't treat mathematics as a serious subject.

SARA: I can't believe that.

TURING: It's true. Do you know what our form-master said the other day? 'This room stinks of mathematics,' he said, looking straight at me, 'go out and get a d-d-disinfectant spray.'

[CHRIS *laughs.*]

SARA: He was joking.

TURING: [*ignoring this*] He hates anything to do with mathematics or science. He once said — and he meant it — he said the Germans lost the Great War because they thought science was more important than religion.

SARA: The teaching of mathematics is not the only way to judge the quality of a school.

TURING: It is as far as I'm concerned.

SARA: Oh, Alan. [*to* CHRIS] I gather you share this enthusiasm for sums and science?

CHRIS: Oh yes, very much so. And it's wonderful having someone like Alan to work with. Has he told you about our experiments?

SARA: A little. Wasn't there something to do with iodine?

TURING: Iodates.

CHRIS: We were trying to examine the time delay in the recombination of ions.

SARA: Yes, it was all far beyond my grasp, I'm afraid. Fascinating, but beyond my grasp. [*to* TURING] It was the same with that theory you were telling me about — what was it? — you know, the man with the Jewish name.

TURING: Einstein.

SARA: Einstein, yes: I didn't understand a word of it — not one word. I only wish I did. Does your family understand these things?

CHRIS: Well, yes — up to a point.

TURING: Morcom's brother is a scientist. They've got their own laboratory at home.

SARA: Really?

TURING: And he's got his own telescope.

SARA: Really? — How splendid.

CHRIS: It's tremendous, Mrs Turing — absolutely terrific. The other night — [*to* TURING] — did I tell you? — the other night, I actually saw one of Jupiter's satellites coming out from eclipse. It was amazing. It was a wonderfully clear night. Absolutely cloudless. I felt I was wandering through the universe. Jupiter, Sirius, Betelgeuse, the Andromeda nebula. It was quite overwhelming. The hugeness of creation.

TURING: Gosh, how terrific.

SARA: Yes, it all sounds very thrilling, I must say. But I do hope you don't frighten your family the way Alan does.

[TURING *sighs with irritation.*]

CHRIS: Frighten them how?

SARA: He got up at three o'clock in the morning last Thursday — I can't imagine why — I woke up and heard footsteps on the stairs. I was convinced that we had burglars in the house, and my husband was on the point of telephoning to the police when we realised that it was only Alan.

TURING: I was mapping the constellations of fixed stars.

[CHRIS *laughs.*]

SARA: I sometimes wish he was interested in stamp collecting or model trains, like other boys.

[TURING *snorts with displeasure;* SARA *rises to her feet;* CHRIS *follows suit.*]

Let's have some tea, shall we? [*to* TURING] Do wash your

hands, they're covered in ink. [*to* CHRIS] Did Alan tell you about my grandfather's cousin? He was a scientist. He invented the electron.

TURING: He didn't invent it, mother; electrons exist, you can't invent them.

SARA: Well, he found them, or discovered them, or something like that. He was a Fellow of the Royal Society. Very distinguished. [*to* TURING, *as she exits*] Do wash your hands.

[TURING *grimaces to* CHRIS.]

TURING: Sorry, Morcom — one can't choose one's own mother.

CHRIS: [*a grin*] She's all right.

[*Brief pause.* TURING *takes a step towards* CHRIS.]

TURING: Do you know what I wish?

CHRIS: What?

TURING: I wish this was my house. My own house. Then we could live here, you and I. We could have our own rooms, our own laboratories. We could work together. Share everything. What a w-w-wonderful life that would be.

[CHRIS *looks at* TURING.]

CHRIS: Yes. Yes, it would.

SARA: [*off*] Come along, Christopher!

CHRIS: I'd better go.

[CHRIS *turns to leave.*]

TURING: Chris.

[CHRIS *pauses.*]

Thank you for c-c-coming to see me.

[CHRIS *smiles.*]

CHRIS: Don't forget to wash your hands.

[CHRIS *exits.*]

[*Lighting change: winter evening.*]

SCENE THREE

TURING *sits at a table.*

RON MILLER *enters. He is about 20, north-country, working-class. He is holding a mug of beer. He looks at* TURING, *hesitates for a moment, then strolls to the table.*

RON: Anyone sitting here?

TURING: No.

[RON *sits; drinks some beer; looks around.*]

RON: Quiet tonight.

TURING: Yes. Very.

RON: All the pubs are the same. I've just been down The King's Head. Same as this place. Nobody round.

TURING: Perhaps it's the weather.

RON: Yeah. Bloody cold.

TURING: Real Christmas weather.

RON: Bloody Christmas. [*drinks*] Christmas in Manchester: the bleedin' bitter end.

[TURING *smiles. Brief pause.*]

TURING: I saw you in here last week.

RON: Yeah, could be. Yeah — I often come in here. God knows why. Quiet as the bloody grave. [*drinks*] I should've stayed at The King's Head. They've got a juke-box down there. That livens it up a bit. All the latest hits. Johnnie Ray, Guy Mitchell, Frankie Laine. [*pause*] Perry Como, Rosemary Clooney, Nat King Cole. [*pause*] Still, it's handy here.

TURING: Handy for work?

RON: No, no — just — you know — handy.

[*Pause.* RON *drinks.*]

TURING: Where do you work?

RON: I don't. Not at the moment. I had a job making spectacle frames. Then the bloody government starts making cuts. No more free teeth and glasses on the National Health. Bang goes the job. Bye-bye, they said — piss off.

TURING: That's bad luck.

RON: You're telling me. So I'm stuck at home. Not much fun in that. [*drinks*] What about you?

TURING: I've got my own place.

RON: I meant your job.

TURING: I'm at the university.

RON: Bit old for that, aren't you?

TURING: I'm on the staff.

RON: A teacher?

TURING: Not exactly. I do, um . , well, research.

RON: What sort?

TURING: Scientific. Mathematics. How's your drink?

RON: Fine.

TURING: Actually, we're trying to build a special sort of machine. What people call the Electronic Brain.

RON: [*stares at* TURING] Bloody hell, that sounds a bit . . .

TURING: A bit what?

RON: Sounds like that film.

TURING: What film?

RON: Michael Rennie. I saw it when I was down in London. Michael Rennie and some sort of robot. [*remembering*] *The Day the Earth Stood Still.* Did you see it?

TURING: No.

RON: Bloody good. [*drinks*] So what's it do, this thing you're making?

TURING: You give it problems — mathematical problems — and it solves them very quickly.

RON: How quickly?

TURING: Very, very quickly. Far more quickly than a man could.

RON: Like an adding machine?

TURING: No, it's more than that. We're trying to make a m-m-machine that can learn things and eventually think for itself.

RON: Think for itself . . . ?

TURING: Why not?

RON: Bloody hell.

TURING: It's not a robot — and it's not really a brain. Not like the human brain, anyway. It's what we call a digital computer.

[*Brief pause.* RON *looks at* TURING.]

RON: You thought this up, did you?

TURING: Sort of.

RON: Must be interesting, a job like that.

TURING: It is.

RON: Yeah, must be. Good money, too, I bet.

TURING: Not bad.

[RON *drinks. Brief pause.*]

RON: I once fancied being a chemist. Must've been about 14. Don't know why. Just fancied the idea of it somehow.

TURING: Did you do anything about it?

RON: Bought myself a chemistry set. Blew the bloody windows out. That was the end of that.

[TURING *smiles.* RON *drinks. Pause.*]

TURING: Look, um . . . would you like something to eat? There's a cafe across the road.

RON: Can't really, not now, I —

TURING: [*quickly, not wishing to be snubbed*] Right.

[*Brief pause.* RON *glances at* TURING.]

RON: How about some other time?

TURING: Yes, all right. When?

RON: Don't mind.

TURING: This weekend?

RON: If you like.

TURING: What about Friday evening?

RON: Okay.

TURING: C-c-come to my house.

RON: [*a brief hesitation*] Okay.

> [TURING *takes a scrap of paper from his pocket and writes his address.*]

TURING: This is the address. Come to my house.

> [*He gives the note to* RON.]

Do you know where it is?

RON: I can find it.

TURING: Come about seven. I'll cook you a meal.

RON: Good cook, are you?

TURING: Not bad. [*smiles*] What's your name?

RON: Ron

TURING: Alan.

> [RON *finishes his beer; he stands up.*]

RON: Okay, Alan — I'll see you Friday.

TURING: About seven.

RON: About seven.

TURING: Don't change your mind.

RON: [*a grin*] I'll be there.

> [RON *exits.* TURING *remains seated.*]

[*Lighting change: winter afternoon.*]

SCENE FOUR

ROSS *enters.*

ROSS: We're having a bit of a problem with regard to this brush salesman you were telling us about.

TURING: Oh?

ROSS: We spoke to some of your neighbours. No one seems to have seen him but you. I don't understand it.

TURING: Perhaps they were out when he called.

ROSS: All of them?

TURING: It's p-p-possible.

ROSS: And we checked with the local domestic appliance firms. None of them have had a salesman working in your area.

TURING: Well, as I said, I might've been mistaken.

ROSS: What about?

TURING: What he was doing, what he was selling.

ROSS: I can't believe you'd make a mistake like that, sir. You must've been talking to him for several minutes. At least. Weren't you?

TURING: As I recall, I was rather preoccupied. I was working, you see, and, uh . . . well, to be honest, I don't remember much about him.

ROSS: What did he look like? You must remember what he looked like.

TURING: Not really.
[*Pause.* ROSS *waits.*]
Youngish. Ordinary. I didn't take much notice of him.

ROSS: You didn't, did you, sir?

TURING: Well, no.

ROSS: Why not?

TURING: He was only a t-t-travelling salesman, after all.

ROSS: Even so . . . all that talk about burglars and suspicious characters — I'd have made sure I knew what he looked like.

TURING: Perhaps that's because you're a policeman.

ROSS: Could be.

TURING: Anyway, why is he so important? Surely it's the burglar you should be looking for.

ROSS: Supposing he wasn't a brush salesman. Supposing he was somehow involved in the burglary.

TURING: [*a hint of alarm*] What makes you think that?

ROSS: He might even be the burglar. It's an old trick: he knocks on the door, if no one answers, in he goes. The brush salesman story is just camouflage.

TURING: That doesn't make sense.

ROSS: Why not?

TURING: If he was involved in the b-b-burglary, why should he pretend to warn me?

ROSS: [*a shrug*] People do funny things.

TURING: Oh look, this is ridiculous. I feel I'm making a f-f-fuss about nothing. I didn't lose very much, well hardly anything. I can't think why I bothered to report it.

ROSS: I'm glad you did, sir. All crimes should be reported: big and small.

TURING: It all seems so trivial.

ROSS: Trivial . . . ?

TURING: Don't you think?

ROSS: Well, that's our problem now, so don't you worry about it. Okay?

TURING: [*a reluctant nod*] If you say so.

ROSS: Good. [*goes to the door*] If you remember anything — no matter how trivial it may seem — I'd be grateful if you'd let me know.

TURING: All right.

[ROSS *opens the door for* TURING.]

ROSS: You won't be leaving Manchester, will you, sir?

TURING: [*a frown*] How do you mean?

ROSS: Just in case I need to talk to you.

TURING: Oh, no — no, no . . . well, I'll be in London next week, j-j-just for a couple of days.

ROSS: When?

TURING: Tuesday and Wednesday. I'm doing a broadcast.

ROSS: Oh really?

TURING: A talk — you know — a discussion.

ROSS: What about?

TURING: Er — machines. Can machines think? Is it possible to build a machine that thinks for itself?

ROSS: Sounds interesting. When's it on?

TURING: Tuesday evening, Third programme, eight o'clock.

ROSS: Well, I'll listen. Make a point of it.

[*He shakes* TURING *by the hand.*]

Thanks very much, Mr Turing. I'll give you a ring if anything turns up.

TURING: Thank you.

[TURING *exits.*]

[JOHN SMITH *enters: middle-aged, wearing a dark city suit; his voice is authoritative; upper-class.*]

SMITH: What do you think?

ROSS: A bit of a joke, him doing a broadcast with a stammer like that.

SMITH: About the burglary.

ROSS: I'm not sure, sir. It doesn't add up, somehow. He's not telling us everything.

SMITH: Do you think he's lying?

ROSS: I think he might be.

[SMITH *considers this for a moment; then he goes to the door;* ROSS *follows.*]

SMITH: Let me know what happens. Your superintendent knows where to find me.

ROSS: Yes, sir.

SMITH: Handle it carefully, Ross; carefully and discreetly.

ROSS: Yes, sir.

SMITH: There are certain anxieties. The Foreign Office wants to avoid any possible embarrassment.

ROSS: [*surprised*] I didn't know he was mixed up with the Foreign Office.

SMITH: He got to be their chap during the war. Quite a big fish, our Mr Turing. The P.M. thought the world of him.

[SMITH *and* ROSS *exit.*]

[*Lighting change: autumn afternoon.*]

SCENE FIVE

TURING *enters with* DILLWYN KNOX.

KNOX *is about 60; Eton and King's; walks with a slight limp. He is carrying a bulky file.*

KNOX: So you found us all right?

TURING: Yes, thank you, no problems.

KNOX: Silly question, really. I mean, here you are. Of course you found us. [*puts the file on a table*] Punctual to the minute. Bravo. That's quite an achievement these days. If only Churchill could take a leaf out of Mussolini's book and make the trains run on time. Which one did you catch?

TURING: I got here this morning, actually.

KNOX: This morning?

TURING: I didn't want to be late.

KNOX: You've been here all day?

TURING: Yes.

KNOX: Oh dear, poor you. Bletchley doesn't have much to offer — as you must've discovered.

TURING: I went to the cinema.

KNOX: Well, exactly. Nothing else to do here. What did you see?

TURING: A cartoon film: *Snow White and the Seven Dwarfs.*

KNOX: I think I saw it; I took one of my nieces. Isn't there a wicked witch?

TURING: Yes, she gives Snow White a poisoned apple.

KNOX: Don't tell me it's got a sad ending.

TURING: No, she wakes up in the arms of a handsome prince. It's really quite t-t-touching. In a sentimental sort of way.

KNOX: Obviously I wasn't paying enough attention. I must make a point of seeing it again sometime.

[*He sits;* TURING *sits.*]

You must be wondering what this is all about.

TURING: Well, I know your reputation as a code-breaker, Mr Knox; I assumed it was something to do with the deciphering work you're doing here.

KNOX: Ah. You've heard about that.

TURING: Nothing much, just talk.

KNOX: What sort of talk?

TURING: Amongst my c-c-colleagues at Cambridge.

[KNOX *rises to his feet, clearly disconcerted.*]

KNOX: It's supposed to be tremendously secret, this place — I mean quite tremendously secret. Hence all the barbed wire and soldiers and passwords and so on.

TURING: Yes, I realise that.

KNOX: How did you get in, by the way? Did they tell you the password?

TURING: I showed them your letter.

KNOX: Oh good, well done. [*sits*] I always make a frightful balls-up of this password nonsense. It must be something to do with my age.

TURING: In what respect?

KNOX: Failing memory. We all live far too long, that's the trouble: faculties fade, the body disintegrates, the mind crumbles. My solicitor says that dentists are to blame. He opines that Nature intended us to die as soon as our teeth drop out; but thanks to the advances in dentistry we struggle on into an infirm and wretched old age. [*brief pause*] Yes . . . ?

TURING: I didn't speak.

KNOX: What was I saying?

TURING: Passwords.

KNOX: Ah yes. We're supposed to call this place Station X, but of course everyone knows it's the Government Code and Cipher School: The G.C.C.S. — waggishly referred to as the Golf Club and Chess Society.

[*He laughs;* TURING *smiles.* KNOX *opens the file.*]

You'll have to bear with me, Turing; I'm not an administrator, neither am I a mathematician — but since it seems highly likely that we shall be working together, the powers-that-be think we should have some sort of exploratory conversation. Is that all right with you?

TURING: Of course.

KNOX: Good. [*indicates the file*] This is your file. I shall consult it from time to time. There's no need to be alarmed.

TURING: I'm not.

KNOX: Good. [*looks at the file*] So you went to Sherborne, King's — [*some surprise*] — and then America: 1936 to 1938; two years in America. How was that? Did you enjoy Princeton?

TURING: Well, yes, it was . . . yes.

KNOX: Enjoy is scarcely the right word, perhaps.

TURING: No, no, as a m-m-matter of fact it was very enjoyable, very stimulating.

KNOX: What exactly did you do there?

TURING: Um . . . well, I'd just published a p-p-paper on Computable Numbers, and I was able to develop some of those ideas and, uh . . . various other things, various other research projects.

KNOX: All concerned with mathematics and logic?

TURING: Yes.

KNOX: Yes. [*turning a page*] And your interest in codes and ciphers: how did that begin?

TURING: I've always been interested, I think, ever since I was a boy. I got a prize at school: a book called 'M-m-mathematical Recreations and Essays'. There was a chapter on cryptography. I found it fascinating; and I suppose it awakened my interest — focussed my interest — in ciphers. And then, much more recently, when I came back from America, I realised that my ideas in mathematics and logic might be applied to ciphers. That, of course, created something of a dilemma.

KNOX: Why?

TURING: I knew that such knowledge would acquire military value if war were declared. I was concerned about the moral implications of putting my, ah — intellectual armoury — at the disposal of a g-g-government at war.

KNOX: Have you managed to resolve this dilemma?

TURING: Well, I'm here. Doesn't that answer your question?

KNOX: Not necessarily. I gather you were a supporter of the Anti-War movement at Cambridge?

TURING: In 1933, yes.

KNOX: Would you describe yourself as a pacifist?

TURING: No, I wouldn't.

KNOX: You've changed your mind?

TURING: No, I've always thought that some wars could be justified.

KNOX: Justified how?

TURING: As a lesser evil in the last resort. Hitler has brought us to that last resort.

KNOX: So you would regard this war as a necessary evil?

TURING: F-f-first and foremost, I regard this war as a most unfortunate interruption to my work. But also — yes, you're right — I do think of it as a necessary evil.

KNOX: What about loyalty to your country — a sense of duty? Do these considerations carry any weight with you?

TURING: [*bristling*] As it happens, I have a deep and p-p-passionate love of my country — but whenever I hear people appealing to my loyalty or duty I feel that I'm being made to do something I don't want to do. [*firmly*] I have come here because I have decided for myself what I should do in the, uh . . . current circumstances. I think I'd be more useful here than on a b-b-battlefield.

[KNOX *looks at him. Brief pause.*]

KNOX: A word of warning. Do not imagine that the nature of the work we do will protect you from the moral responsibility for killing and destruction. Sometimes very hard decisions have to be made [*brief pause*] How do you feel about that?

TURING: I have always been willing — eager, in fact — to accept moral responsibility for what I do.

KNOX: Good. [*a small smile*] Good! [*consulting the file; turning a page*] I've been furnished with some details of your work, Mr Turing, most of which I have to tell you I find almost totally incomprehensible.

TURING: That's hardly surprising.

KNOX: I knew quite a bit about mathematics when I was young, but this is — well, baffling. [*studies file*] Um — for example . . . this thing here: 'On Computable Numbers with an Application to the Ent-scheid-ungs-prob-lem'.

[*He raises his head and looks at* TURING.]

Perhaps you could tell me about it.

TURING: Tell you what?

KNOX: Well, anything — a few words of explanation — in general terms.

[TURING *looks at him. Brief pause.*]

TURING: A few words of explanation?

KNOX: Yes.

TURING: In general terms?

KNOX. If possible.

TURING: It's about right and wrong. In general terms. It's a technical p-p-paper in mathematical logic, but it's also about the difficulty of telling right from wrong. [*brief pause*] People think — most people think — that in mathematics we always know what is right and what is wrong. Not so. Not any more. It's a problem that's occupied mathematicians for forty or fifty years. How can you tell right from wrong? You know Bertrand Russell?

KNOX. We've met.

TURING: Well he's written an immense book about it: 'Principia Mathematica'. His idea was to break down all mathematical concepts and arguments into little bits and then show that they could be derived from pure logic, but it didn't quite work out that way. After many years of intensive work, all he was able to do was to show that it's terribly difficult to do anything of the kind. But it was an important book. Important and influential. It influenced both David Hilbert and Kurt Gödel. [*a brief digression*] You could, I suppose, make a comparison between these preoccupations and what physicists call 'splitting the atom'. As analysing the physical atom has led to the discovery of a new kind of physics, so the attempt to analyse these mathematical atoms has led to a new kind of mathematics. [*resuming the main thread of his explanation*] Hilbert took the whole thing a stage further. I don't suppose his name means m-m-much to you — if anything — but there we are, that's the way of the world; people never seem to hear of the really great mathematicians. Hilbert looked at the problem from a completely different angle, and he said, if we are going to have any fundamental system for mathematics — like the one Russell was trying to work out — it must satisfy three basic requirements: consistency, completeness and decidability. Consistency means that you won't ever get a contradiction in your own system; in other words, you'll never be able to f-f-follow the rules of your system and end up by showing that two and two make five. Completeness means that if any statement is true, there must be some way of proving it by using the rules of your system. And decidability means, uh — decidability means that there must exist some method, some d-d-definite procedure or test, which can be applied to any given assertion and

which will decide whether or not that assertion is provable. Hilbert thought that this was a very reasonable set of
requirements to impose; but within a few years Kurt
Gödel showed that no system for mathematics could be
both consistent and complete. He did this by constructing
a mathematical assertion that said — in effect: 'This
assertion cannot be proved.' A classic paradox. 'This
assertion cannot be proved.' Well either it can be proved
or it can't. If it can be proved we have a contradiction, and
the system is inconsistent. If it cannot be proved then the
assertion is true — but it can't be proved; which means
that the system is incomplete. Thus mathematics is either
inconsistent or it's incomplete. It's a beautiful theorem,
quite b-b-beautiful. Gödel's theorem is the most beautiful thing I know. But the question of decidability was still
unresolved. Hilbert had, as I said, thought there should
be a single clearly defined method for deciding whether
or not mathematical assertions were provable. The decision
problem he called it. 'The Entscheidungsproblem'. In my
paper on computer numbers I showed that there can be
no one method that will work for all questions. Solving
mathematical problems requires an infinite supply of new
ideas. It was, of course, a monumental task to prove such
a thing. One needed to examine the provability of all
mathematical assertions past, present and future. How on
earth could this be done? One word gave me the clue.
People had been talking about the possibility of a mechanical method, a method that could be applied mechani-
cally to solving mathematical problems without requiring
any human intervention or ingenuity. Machine! — that
was the crucial word. I conceived the idea of a machine, a
Turing Machine, that would be able to scan mathematical
symbols — to read them if you like — to read a mathematical assertion and to arrive at the verdict as to whether
or not that assertion is provable. With this concept I was
able to prove that Hilbert was wrong. My idea worked.

KNOX: You actually built this machine?

TURING: No, of course not. It was a machine of the imagination,
like one of Einstein's thought experiments. Building it
wasn't important; it's a perfectly clear idea, after all.

KNOX: Yes, I see; well, I don't, but I see something. I think.

[*He looks at* TURING.]

Forgive me for asking a crass and naive question — but

what is the point of devising a machine that cannot be built in order to prove that there are certain mathematical statements that cannot be proved? Is there any practical value in all this?

TURING: The possibilities are boundless — this is only the beginning. In my paper I explain how a special kind of Turing machine — I call it the Universal Machine — could carry out any mental process whatsoever.
[*Pause.*]

KNOX: [*a small smile*] The originality of your thinking is clearly remarkable; and I'm sure that you'll prove to be an invaluable member of our team, group, call it what you will. [*closes the file*] We'd like you to start work immediately. Is that all right?

TURING: Of course.

KNOX: Are there any questions you want to ask me?

TURING: Not really; my only anxiety is about my f-f-fitting into a place like this. I've never been very good at organising things — least of all myself — and I'm not too sure how well I'll function in a government department.

KNOX: You mustn't worry about that. There's a healthy disregard of organisational formality at G.C.C.S. — if there weren't, I wouldn't be here. As far as I'm concerned, rules are only important in cricket, poetry and the scholarly editing of ancient texts. [*smiles; rises to his feet*] I'm going to ask Miss Green to join us. [*goes to the door and opens it*] Will you ask Pat to come in, please? [*returns to his chair*] Patricia Green is one our most able cryptanalysts. Quite as good as any chap.

TURING: What sort of work shall I be doing?

KNOX: You'll be concentrating on something called the Enigma code. It's been devised and developed by the Germans — and it's an absolute pig.
[PAT *appears at the door.*]
Ah — Pat. Do come in.
[*She enters.*]
Come and meet Alan Turing.
[TURING *and* PAT *shake hands.*]

PAT: How do you do.

TURING: How do you do.

KNOX: You'll be working with Pat and Gordon Welchman. Have you found him somewhere to live?

PAT: The Crown Inn at Shenley Brook End.

KNOX: Oh good — that's only about three miles away. [*to* TUR-ING] Have you got a bicycle? You'll need a bicycle. [*to* PAT] I shall rely on you to tell Mr Turing about the Enigma.

PAT: Yes, of course.

KNOX: The point is, this damn code is a vital part of the Nazi war effort — vital. The army uses it, so does the Luftwaffe, and — most importantly — so do the U-boats. And if the U-boats get control of the north Atlantic, our merchant ships won't stand a chance. They'll starve us out. So — the Enigma's got to be broken.

TURING: What type of code is it?

> [KNOX *is gathering together his scattered papers and putting them back into the file.*]

PAT: Mechanical.

KNOX: Which puts the ball firmly in your court.

PAT: They have a machine which substitutes one letter for another but there are thousands of millions of ways the substitutions can be made depending on how it's set up each day. Basically our problem is one of solving equations with permutation groups.

TURING: Do you know what the permutations· are?

KNOX: First things first. Go back to Cambridge. Pack your bags. Pat will give you a guided tour on Monday morning. [*picks up the file and goes to the door*] Bletchley was chosen by the G.C.C.S. because it's equidistant from Oxford and Cambridge. I should warn you that the unexpected influx of academics and intellectuals has put a severe strain on local resources. You'll find it very difficult to get pipe tobacco or copies of *The Times*.

> [KNOX *exits.* PAT *follows him to the door but then pauses.*]

PAT: Actually, we've met before.

TURING: Have we? When?

PAT: You read a paper to the Moral Science Club at Cambridge. We met briefly afterwards.

TURING: That must've been — when?

PAT: December 1933. I remember it very clearly. I remember you saying that mathematical propositions had not just one but a variety of interpretations. You opened up all sorts of possibilities I'd never thought of before. It was most exciting.

TURING: [*a smile*] Thank you.

[Brief pause. PAT *manages another hesitant smile.]*

PAT: Well — I'll see you on Monday.

TURING: Yes, fine, I'll look forward to it.

*[*PAT *exits.]*

[Lighting change: winter morning.]

SCENE SIX

TURING *goes to the table; he takes off his jacket and hangs it on the back of a chair; he sits down.*

RON *enters; he is wearing only trousers and shoes; he stands in the doorway, rubbing the sleep out of his eyes.*

RON: What's the time?

TURING: Nine o'clock.

*[*RON *yawns.]*

RON: Bit of a bloody mess.

TURING: What is?

RON: This house. *[walks to the table]* What's all that stuff in the bathroom? Doesn't half stink.

TURING: I'm trying to make some weed-killer.

RON: What for?

TURING: To kill weeds.

RON: Why don't you buy some? You could afford it.

TURING: I like making things. It's fun.

*[*RON *sits at the table.]*

Did you sleep all right?

RON: Not bad.

[Pause. He looks at TURING.*]*

Do you often do this?

TURING: Do what?

RON: Have blokes back here.

TURING: Not often.

*[*RON *yawns. Pause.]*

RON: Have you always been queer?

TURING: Yes.

RON: Never fancied girls?

TURING: No.

RON: I like a bit of both, myself. I'd rather have a girl, given the chance, but they're not so easy to get, not when you're skint. [*pause*] Some real old queen picked me up when I was in London. Silk sheets, mirror over the bed. A bit different to this place.

[RON *grins. Pause.*]

TURING: You were t-t-talking in your sleep.

RON: Was I? What did I say?

TURING: I couldn't make it out. You seemed frightened of something.

RON: I was having a dream. [*pause*] It's funny: I've had the same dream over and over again, ever since I was a kid.

TURING: What is it?

RON: Well, it's more of a nightmare, really. It's as if I'm in some huge empty space; sort of floating there, you know, just floating in mid-air in this great dark empty space. And suddenly, ever so quiet at first, a strange noise begins. Can't describe it. It's the sort of noise you can feel all through your body, and I start trembling, I can feel myself trembling with the noise, and as the noise gets louder I tremble more and more and start to shake, and it gets louder and louder, and there's nothing I can do to stop it, nothing.

[*Pause.*]

TURING: What happens then?

RON: That's it. That's all. Then I wake up. [*grins*] Pretty spooky, eh?

[*No response. Pause.*]

You don't half snore.

TURING: Sorry.

RON: Just like my Dad. You can hear him snoring all over the bloody house.

TURING: What were you doing in London?

RON: How do you mean?

TURING: Were you working, having a holiday, or what?

RON: Sort of holiday, I suppose. I hitched a lift down to see the Festival of Britain. Bloody good. Did you go?

TURING: Yes.

RON: Like it?

TURING: It was all right.

RON: Bloody good, I thought. Anyway, I tried to get a job down there but nothing worked out. [*brief pause*] I got nicked pinching food from Sainsbury's. They sent me back here on probation.

[*No response. Pause.* RON *yawns.*]

What's that place down the road?

TURING: What place?

RON: That big shed. You can see it from the bedroom window.

TURING: It's an old R.A.F. hangar.

RON: I didn't know the R.A.F. was up here.

TURING: They were during the war.

RON: Were you here then?

> [TURING *shakes his head.*]

Where were you?

TURING: Around and about.

RON: Doing what?

TURING: Working for the g-g-government.

RON: Doing what?

TURING: I was a — [*the double-bluff is perfectly judged*] — I was a code-breaker.

RON: [*staring*] A what?

TURING: A code-breaker. I deciphered all the German codes and won the war singlehandedly. That's top secret, of course, nobody knows.

RON: [*grinning*] Just me.

TURING: You and Mr Churchill.

> [RON *laughs;* TURING *grins.*]

I'll tell you something else.

RON: What's that?

TURING: That, um — that hangar down the road: it grows b-b-bigger at night.

RON: You're barmy.

TURING: It does. You look.

RON: Barmy!

TURING: It seems to, anyway. In the daytime it's just an ordinary large shed, but when the sun goes down it seems to get bigger and bigger. I'm thinking of writing a story about it.

RON: [*playing along*] Good idea.

TURING: Do you think so?

RON: Why not?

TURING: It's rather like that film you enjoyed so much.

RON: The one about the robot?

TURING: Yes. It's quite creepy, actually, quite spooky. I imagine that I go inside the hangar; it's deserted, derelict, very dark — you can't see a thing. And as I go in, the door bangs shut behind me.

RON: No way out.

TURING: No way out. Then — then I realise that it's not a hangar at all. I'm trapped inside an enormous mechanical brain. And this brain, the hangar, starts to p-p-play chess with me. And I've got to win, otherwise I'll never get out. All day and all night, we play; all the next day and all the next night. But the b-b-brain's too clever for me, I can't keep up with the moves — and I'm terrified I'll be trapped there for the rest of my life. [*brief pause; grins*] The trouble is, I can't think of a good ending.

RON: Flash Gordon comes in and rescues you.

[TURING *smiles.*]

TURING: I thought perhaps I could find a p-p-piece of chalk and write a few sums on the wall: very easy sums, simple arithmetic, that sort of thing; and I'd do them deliberately badly, make silly mistakes; I'd do them so slowly and so badly that the brain would get more and more despairing and then, f-f-finally . . .

RON: What?

TURING: The brain commits suicide. [*pause*] What do you think of that?

TURING: Flash Gordon's better.

TURING: [*a smile*] Maybe.

[RON *stands up.*]

RON: Got any tea?

TURING: In the kitchen.

[RON *exits. Brief pause.* RON *returns.*]

RON: There's no milk.

TURING: Sorry.

RON: No tea either, just coffee.

TURING: We'll have some breakfast later.

RON: I'm starving. Aren't there any shops around here?

TURING: There's a place at the end of the road.

RON: I'll nip down, shall I? Got any money?

TURING: Put your shoes on, I'll find some.

RON: Right.

[RON *exits.*]

[TURING *takes his wallet from his jacket pocket. He is clearly surprised by what he finds inside. He recounts the bank notes, checking them carefully. He rises to his feet.*]

[RON *enters, now wearing a sweater and a wind-cheater.*]

I'll get some tea and milk. How about some bacon?

TURING: Have you been taking m-m-money from my wallet?

RON: What?

TURING: You heard.

RON: I haven't touched your bloody wallet.

TURING: I had fifteen p-p-pounds yesterday, there's only seven left.

RON: It's nothing to do with me.

TURING: Where's it gone then?

RON: How should I know?

TURING: Give it back.

RON: I haven't got it!

TURING: I don't believe you.

RON: All right, search me —

TURING: Don't be ridiculous.

RON: — come on, search me.

TURING: You've hidden it somewhere.

RON: What the fuck are you talking about?

> [*Brief pause.* TURING *and* RON *stand facing each other.*]

Look, why should I take money from you?

TURING: You said you were hard up.

RON: I didn't.

TURING: You said you were out of work.

RON: So what?

TURING: Please, Ron, give it back.

RON: Piss off!

TURING: Give it back and we'll say no more about it.

RON: I'm not a bloody thief!

TURING: You just said you were. You said you're on probation.

RON: If you think I nicked that money, call the police.

> [TURING *does not move.*]

Come on, there's the phone — what are you waiting for? [*grabs the telephone receiver*] Come on!

TURING: Put it down.

RON: Come on!

> [TURING *does not move.* RON *throws the telephone receiver onto the floor and strides angrily across the room.* TURING *stands motionless, looking at him. Pause.*]

TURING: I'm sorry. I'm sorry. [*picks up the receiver and replaces it on the telephone*] I lost my temper. I'm sorry.

> [*No response.*]

    Perhaps I made a mistake.

RON: Fucking nerve!

TURING: I'm sorry.

        [RON *goes to the door.*]

    Where are you going?

RON: I'm not bloody staying here.

TURING: Please don't go.

RON: [*girlish, mocking him*] Please don't go.

TURING: I must've been mistaken. I'm sorry.

        [*No response.*]

    I thought I had fifteen pounds. Maybe I didn't. Let's forget it, shall we? [*takes some money from his wallet*] G-g-go and get us some breakfast.

RON: [*mimicking him*] G-g-get it yourself.

TURING: I've said I'm sorry.

RON: So what?

TURING: Let's be friends.

        [*Pause.* TURING *takes a step towards* RON.]

    Do you want some money? Do you?

        [RON *almost replies; hesitates.*]

    How much do you need?

RON: I'm not a bloody renter.

TURING: I know. [*brief pause*] If you're hard up, if you want some money, you've only got to ask.

        [*Brief pause.*]

RON: Call it a loan, then.

TURING: How much?

RON: Three?

        [TURING *takes three pound notes from his wallet and gives them to* RON.]

TURING: Shall I see you again?

RON: Maybe. Yeah, maybe.

TURING: Perhaps I'll see you in the pub.

RON: Yeah. [*brief pause*] I'd better go.

TURING: Have some breakfast first. Tea and b-b-bacon. [*offers more money for food*] Have some breakfast, then go. I'll cook you bacon and eggs.

        [RON *hestitates.*]

RON: I can't stay long.

TURING: I know.

RON: Okay. [*takes the money*] Where's this shop? Down the road?

TURING: Down the road, turn left.
> [ROM *exits.* TURING *puts on his jacket.*]

> [*Lighting change: summer afternoon; shadows of foliage.*]

SCENE SEVEN

> SARA *and* PAT *enter; they are wearing summer clothes.* SARA *is carrying a tray with a jug and three glasses. She puts the tray on a table.*

SARA: There are no oranges and no lemons, so we've made a fruit cocktail out of apples and pears.

PAT: It tastes very nice.

TURING: It's a depressing colour.

SARA: Don't start finding fault. Things are difficult enough these days. [*pours the drink into the glasses*] Pat's coming to church with me.

TURING: Oh good.

SARA: [*giving a glass to* TURING] Do come, Alan, dear.

TURING: Not today. [*sipping the drink*] Ugh.

PAT: What's the matter?

TURING: It's terribly sour.

PAT: Is it?

TURING: Try some.

PAT: I already have.

SARA: What's that drink made from pears? Is it called perry?

PAT: Yes, I think so.

SARA: Well, this is a combination of cider and perry.

PAT: Ciderry.

SARA: Perryder.
> [*They laugh.*]

I'm so glad you were able to come down today. I was afraid there might've been a last minute change of plans.

PAT: I've been looking forward to it.

SARA: Have you, dear? So have I. It's so seldom that Alan invites his friends to see us. Hardly ever, in fact. Of course it was different when he was at school. His friend Chris used to come most holidays. Such a charming boy. And a very nice family.

TURING: I don't think Pat wants to hear about my b-b-boyhood relationships.

SARA: Why not? It's always interesting to learn something about people you're fond of. [*smiles at* PAT] I do envy your having gone to Cambridge. When I was young it was considered a waste of time to give a girl a good education. And if you did show any sign of intellectual ability, you were always afraid of being called a blue stocking. It was really most unfair. [*offering to refill* PAT*'s glass*] Would you like some more?

PAT: Please.

SARA: [*to* TURING, *as she pours the drink*] Do come to church, Alan; it'd be so nice if we all went together.

TURING: What's the point?

SARA: Does there have to be a point?

TURING: It seems idiotic for a non-believer to spend his S-s-sunday evening in church.

SARA: You're not a non-believer.

TURING: I am.

SARA: You used not to be. [*to* PAT] He was once extremely devout.

TURING: You never understood what I thought.

SARA: [*briskly*] Maybe not. [*quickly addressing* PAT] Is your father Church of England?

PAT: Yes. His parish is in Wiltshire.

SARA: It's always been a day-dream of mine to live in an ivy-covered vicarage, deep in the country, with oaks and elms and a distant view of a lovely Norman church.

TURING: [*raising his glass*] This needs some sugar. Do you have any sugar?

SARA: We only get eight ounces a week. Or doesn't rationing apply to people like you?

TURING: People like me . . . ?

SARA: One's always hearing about people in hush-hush jobs living off the fat of the land.

TURING: [*to* PAT] Would you say we lived off the fat of the land?

PAT: [*smiles*] Hardly.

TURING: Absolutely not. [*to* SARA] And stop fishing.

SARA: Fishing . . . ?

TURING: All these hints about hush-hush jobs; you know p-p-perfectly well we can't tell you what we do.

SARA: All right, don't be cross. [*turns to leave*] I'll go and see if we've got any sugar.

[SARA *exits. Pause.*]

PAT: She's quite right, you know.

TURING: What about?

PAT: I do like hearing about your family and friends. I wish you talked about them.

TURING: I do sometimes.

PAT: Apart from anything else, it's embarrassing. I had no idea your father was ill until your mother mentioned it.

TURING: He's not ill; he's in p-p-poor health. He had a prostate operation some years ago, and he's been vaguely off-colour ever since. And my brother's in the army, by the way — just to complete the picture; he's in the army, in Egypt.

PAT: Yes, I know.

TURING: I suppose my mother told you.

PAT: Yes.

TURING: Well, since she tells you everything, there's no need for me to d-d-duplicate the information.

[*He looks at* PAT; *she says nothing.*]

Well, is there?

PAT: Who's Chris?

TURING: A friend of mine at Sherborne.

PAT: Your mother obviously liked him.

TURING: Yes. [*pause; his irritation recedes*] Yes — he was a remark-able boy. Very clever. Very perceptive. Very . . . mature for his age. He made everyone else seem so ordinary. [*brief pause*] It was one of those intense f-f-friendships that only happen when you're young. [*brief pause*] I wor-shipped the ground he walked on.

[PAT *looks at him; he seems anxious to avoid her gaze.*]

PAT: Have you kept in touch?

TURING: He died. [*brief pause*] He'd had T.B. when he was a small boy. I didn't know that. He never told me. He hadn't really recovered. [*brief pause*] He was taken ill at school. We were all asleep. The next morning I heard he'd been rushed to hospital. He died six days later. Thursday, February 13th, 1930. I was d-d-devastated.

[*Pause.* TURING *sips his fruit drink.*]

PAT: Poor Alan.

[TURING *looks at her; a shy hesitation before he speaks.*]

TURING: I felt . . . I felt I should've died and not him; and that the only possible excuse for living was that I should achieve something Chris could no longer do. [*brief pause*] I used to think . . . after he d-d-died, I almost believed that he was still with me in spirit and could help me. [*a wry smile*] It was that, I think, that gave my mother the impression that I was devoutly religious. It wasn't that at all. I was obsessed with the idea — with the question — whether or not Christopher's mind could exist without his b-b-body. It was an obsession that stayed with me for many years. What are mental processes? Can they take place in something other than a living brain? In a way — in a very real way — many of the problems I've tried to solve in my work lead directly b-b-back to Chris. [*smiles*] Wouldn't he be amused?

PAT: I think he'd be pleased.

TURING: I hope so.

> [*Pause.* PAT *touches his hand: a gentle, fleeting gesture.*]

PAT: Why don't you come to church? It'd give your mother so much pleasure.

> [TURING *moves away from her.*]

TURING: It would be a lie. Like pretending this ghastly drink isn't ghastly. [*puts the glass on the table*] Ugh!

PAT: It's a pretty harmless pretence.

TURING: Most pretence is self-deluding, and that's far from harmless. [*animated*] Just look at all our confrères at Bletchley — everyone pretending to be so radiantly optimistic! Why do it — why? What's the point?

PAT: It's better than being gloomy all the time.

TURING: Is it? [*brief pause*] I worked out the chances of our being able to crack the U-boat Enigma. Guess what they are.

PAT: Well, I suppose it must be something like —

TURING: [*cutting in*] Fifty-thousand-to-one against.

PAT: We might be lucky.

TURING: P-p-pigs might fly. [*pause*] And I've been wondering what would happen if we lost the war — how we'd survive.

PAT: Don't think about such things.

TURING: We've got to, otherwise we're just burying our heads in the sand.

PAT: All we can do is live from day to day, everything changes, you know that.

TURING: We ought to make plans.

PAT: Like what?

TURING: Well, I thought of buying some razor blades; they'll be in very short supply if we lose the war, so at least we'd have s-s-something to sell.

> [PAT *stares at him.*]

PAT: Razor blades? How many razor blades?

TURING: Enough to fill a large suitcase.

PAT: [*laughing*] Oh, Prof — you're not serious.

TURING: I certainly am.

PAT: You can't just walk into a chemist's shop and buy hundreds — thousands — of razor blades.

[*No response.*]

Well, can you?

TURING: I don't know. Possibly.

PAT: Well, you can't.

[TURING *looks at her. Brief pause.*]

TURING: I could buy some silver.

PAT: Silver what?

TURING: Lumps of it — ingots, or whatever they're called. If I took some money out of the bank and bought a couple of silver ingots, I could bury them and d-d-dig them up when the war is over.

PAT: Bury them where?

TURING: Anywhere — somewhere at Bletchley.

PAT: [*laughing*] Oh, Alan . . . !

TURING: Why not?

PAT: Oh, Alan.

TURING: I'm serious, I mean it — I've already made some enquiries about buying the silver.

[PAT*'s laughter fades; she is moved by his boyish earnestness; she reaches out and takes him by the hand.*]

PAT: [*tenderly*] Oh, Alan . . .

[*Disturbed by this show of intimacy,* TURING *turns from her abruptly and plunges his hand into his coat pocket; he pulls out a fir cone.*]

TURING: Look at this. It's a fir cone.

PAT: I can see it's a fir cone.

TURING: Take it. Look at it.

[*She does so.*]

I'll tell you something extraordinary about it.

PAT: It looks ordinary enough to me.

TURING: Define what is meant by a Fibonacci sequence.

PAT: A Fibonacci sequence is a sequence of numbers where each is the sum of the previous two: one, then one — then one and one, two — one and two, three — then, two and three, five — then three and five, eight —

TURING: [*continuing the sequence*] — five and eight, thirteen. Well done, full marks. Now look at that fir cone. Look at the pattern of the bracts — the leaves. Follow them spiralling around the cone: eight lines twisting round to the left, thirteen twisting to the right. The numbers always come from the Fibonacci sequence.

PAT: [*examining the fir cone more closely*] Always . . . ?

TURING: Always. And not just fir cones — the petals of most flowers grow in the same way. Isn't that amazing?

PAT: Yes, it is.

TURING: And it prompts the age-old question: is G-g-god a mathematician?

> [TURING *smiles;* PAT *looks at him; she returns the fir cone.*]

PAT: I love you, Prof.

> [*No response.*]

I love you.

> [TURING *puts the fir cone in his pocket.*]

You know that.

TURING: Yes.

PAT: You're supposed to say, 'I love you too.'

TURING: I know.

> [*Pause.*]

PAT: Please say something.

TURING: I don't think of myself as a very lovable person.

PAT: Well, you are.

TURING: There are lots of m-m-men at Bletchley who are much more lovable than me.

PAT: That's where you're wrong.

TURING: Don't be silly, of course there are. I see them every lunchtime, rushing about the lawn, p-p-playing rounders, laughing, looking all fit and healthy and manly. I can't imagine why you haven't fallen in love with one of them.

PAT: Because they're dull, that's why.

TURING: So am I.

PAT: That's where you're wrong. You're untidy and messy and lacking almost all the social graces; your clothes are stained and you bite your nails; you tell the truth when it would be kinder to tell a lie, and you've got no patience with people who bore you. But you are not dull. And I love you.

> [*Pause.*]

TURING: As a matter of fact, I do love you.

PAT: [*not really a question*] As a friend.

TURING: As a friend.

PAT: That might change. [*a sad smile*] Perhaps it might change.

[TURING *goes to* PAT *and takes her by the hand.*]

TURING: I'm a homosexual.

PAT: I know. That doesn't stop me loving you. It needn't stop you loving me.

TURING: It would stop me making love to you. I don't want that sort of life. Neither do you, I'm sure.

[SARA *enters, carrying a bowl of sugar. Seeing* TUR-ING *and* PAT *standing so intimately together, she immediately freezes.*]

SARA: Oh, I'm sorry.

[TURING *and* PAT *spring apart.*]

TURING: [*going to* SARA] Don't bother with the sugar. That drink is undrinkable. I'll make some tea, shall I? Would you like some tea?

[*He takes the sugar bowl from* SARA.]

Give me that. [*to* PAT] Tea or sherry, which would you prefer?

PAT: I don't mind.

TURING: If you're going to church, it had better be tea. You don't want to b-b-breathe alcoholic fumes all over the vicar.

[TURING *exits.* PAT *stands very still, her head bowed.* SARA *looks at her anxiously.*]

SARA: What's the matter?

PAT: Nothing.

SARA: Has Alan said something to upset you?

PAT: No, of course not.

SARA: Sorry. It's none of my business. I'm sorry.

[PAT *attempts a reassuring smile.*]

PAT: Nothing's wrong. I'm perfectly all right.

[SARA *sighs.*]

SARA: He's always been his own worst enemy, always. Even when he was young, even at school. His headmaster at Sherborne called him anti-social, I remember. We were terribly upset.

[PAT *can think of no appropriate response; she turns from* SARA.]

PAT: I'd better get ready for church.

SARA: Don't come if you don't want to.

PAT: No, I'd like to, really. [*picks up the tray of glasses*] I'll take this, shall I?

[PAT *exits.*]

[*Again* SARA *sighs; then she follows* PAT.]

[*Lighting change: winter afternoon.*]

SCENE EIGHT

The rat-a-tat of a front door knocker.

TURING *enters. He is wearing running shorts and a singlet. He opens a door.* ROSS *enters.*

TURING: [*some surprise*] Sergeant Ross.

ROSS: Sorry to bother you at home, sir.

TURING: It's no bother. Please come in.

ROSS: Thank you, sir.

> [TURING *closes the door. He feels obliged to explain his mode of dress.*]

TURING: I've just been, uh . . . I do a bit of running.

ROSS: Ah.

TURING: I can't do as much as I used to, alas. [*small smile*] M-m-middle-age creeping on.

ROSS: What were you: long distance, sprinter, or what?

TURING: Long distance. Three miles. M-m-marathon as well.

ROSS: Three miles! God, I couldn't run three miles when I was 20, let alone now. And as for the marathon . . . !

> [TURING *smiles. He and* ROSS *stand facing each other. Pause.*]

TURING: Do you, um . . . do you want to ask me some more questions?

ROSS: Yes, sir, I do; but first of all, I think we should try to clear up this story of yours.

TURING: What story?

ROSS: The one about a young man coming to your house to sell things; brushes, I think you said . . . ?

TURING: Yes?

ROSS: We have good reason to believe that you were lying.

> [*No response.*]

> Were you lying?

> [TURING *hesitates.*]

TURING: Yes.

ROSS: Why?

TURING: I'm sorry. It was foolish of me.

> [*Brief pause.*]

ROSS: Would you like to tell me what really happened?

TURING: There was no brush salesman. I, uh . . . a friend told me about the burglar. George.

ROSS: A friend . . . ?

TURING: Yes.

ROSS: How did he know about the burglary?

TURING: He didn't know exactly; he g-g-guessed.

ROSS: How did he guess?

TURING: He was having a drink with George, you see; in a milk bar; and, uh . . . he mentioned me, my friend mentioned me, and told George where I lived.

> [ROSS *looks; waits.*]

He'd been to dinner, you see. My friend. He'd been to dinner just a few days before, and he was telling George all about it. And then, um . . . after the burglary — I told my friend what had happened and he said it might've been George. He knew that George was a p-p-petty thief, or whatever the expression is. It was just a guess.

ROSS: Well, your friend was right.

TURING: Was he?

ROSS: C.I.D. officers found some fingerprints in your house. This man George has a criminal record.

TURING: Oh, I see. So that proves it?

> [*No response.*]

Yes, I see.

> [*Brief pause.*]

ROSS: This friend of yours: what's his name?

TURING: Ron. Ron Miller.

ROSS: A colleague at the university?

TURING: Well, no.

ROSS: A social acquaintance?

TURING: In a way.

ROSS: Have you known him long?

TURING: Not really.

ROSS: How long?

TURING: Three or f-f-four weeks.

ROSS: And in those three or four weeks, how many times have you seen him?

TURING: I suppose about once a week.

ROSS: How did you meet?

TURING: Just — you know, casually.

ROSS: He's just a casual, social acquaintance?

TURING: Yes.

ROSS: Not what you'd call a close friend?

TURING: Oh no.

ROSS: So why did you lie to conceal his identity?

TURING: I, um . . . I didn't want to get him into trouble.

ROSS: Why not?

TURING: Well . . .

ROSS: He was, after all, partly responsible for your house being burgled.

TURING: I wouldn't say that.

ROSS: Wouldn't you, sir?

TURING: I wouldn't say responsible.

ROSS: Partly responsible.

TURING: It's difficult to say. I mean, it's difficult to say what his rôle in all this actually was — is.

ROSS: He told George your address.

TURING: Yes.

ROSS: And presumably he knows that George has got a criminal record.

TURING: Well, yes.

ROSS: So why go to all these lengths to protect him?

TURING: [*blurting it out*] The truth is, I'm having an affair with him.
[*Pause.*]

ROSS: With Ron?

TURING: Yes.

ROSS: What sort of an affair?

TURING: Well, the usual sort. I mean g-g-going to bed. Sex.

ROSS: You're having a sexual relationship with this man, Ron?

TURING: Yes.

ROSS: What sort of sexual relationship?

TURING: How many sorts are there?

ROSS: You tell me, sir.

TURING: What exactly do you want to know?

ROSS: I need to understand the precise nature of this sexual relationship.

TURING: You m-m-mean you want to know what we did?

ROSS: That would help.

TURING: Well — since you ask — it wasn't much more than mutual masturbation.

ROSS: Did penetration occur?

TURING: No. [*brief pause*] Look, isn't this all rather off the point? I thought you were trying to establish who had burgled my house?

ROSS: That's part of it, yes.

TURING: 'Part of it' . . . ? Part of what?

ROSS: You've just told me that you've committed a criminal offence. I can't ignore that, can I?

TURING: What criminal offence?

ROSS: Gross indecency.

TURING: Oh, now look — I didn't corrupt him — Ron knew what he was doing — he came to my house — my house, don't forget — he came here p-p-perfectly well aware that we'd almost certainly go to b-b-bed together — it didn't come as any great surprise to him — he's had other homosexual experiences — I mean, it's ludicrous to talk about criminal offences — and, as I say, everything happened here, in p-p-private, in my own house, in private — if I hadn't told you, you wouldn't have known anything about it.

ROSS: But you did tell me.

TURING: Can't you forget about it?

> [*No response.*]

Can't you?

> [*Pause.*]

ROSS: How old is this man, Ron?

TURING: I don't know. Nineteen, twenty.

ROSS: And how old are you, sir?

TURING: Thirty-nine. Does it matter? [*rushing on*] Obviously I shouldn't have told you. I'm always saying things I shouldn't. Surely there's no need to make a f-f-fuss about this? I mean, surely you can forget what I told you. Can't you? It's not asking m-m-much, after all. Please.

> [ROSS *remains silent. Pause.* TURING *paces across the room. Pause.*]

What's the position if I make a statement? Shall I?

ROSS: That's up to you, sir.

> [TURING *hesitates for a moment.*]

TURING: Anyway — all right . . . yes, I'll make a statement. [*looks at* ROSS] You'll want me to go to the police station. I'd better get dressed.

> [TURING *exits briskly.*]

END OF ACT ONE

ACT TWO

SCENE ONE

TURING *enters and addresses the audience.*

TURING: Mr Headmaster, members of the staff, boys. I want you to imagine a bowl of porridge. A bowl of cold porridge. When I was a boy at Sherborne — some twenty-five years ago — we always had porridge for breakfast — every day, winter and summer — or so it seems. And for some unaccountable reason, by the time the porridge reached me it was cold. My friend, Christopher Morcom, was more fortunate; he enjoyed his porridge and ate it heartily. But I always sat there at breakfast, staring into a bowl of cold porridge: grey and soft and wrinkled on top. You must be wondering why I'm telling you this. The Headmaster asked me here to talk about my work with computers, and here I am describing bowls of cold porridge. Well, there's a good reason for it and I'll come to that in a moment. I dare say the word computer is unfamiliar to many of you. It is to a lot of people. But if I said electronic brain — ahh — that's much more interesting. And if I were to ask — can a machine think? — I'm sure you'd all be intrigued to know the answer. But before we can consider that properly I must explain something about computers and how they work. First of all, let me compare a computer with the human brain — which brings us back to our bowl of cold porridge, because that's what a human brain looks like: the same colour, the same texture. A computer is very different. It's big — the size of several large wardrobes all joined together; it's hard and metallic on the outside and terribly complicated on the inside, with lots of valves and condensers — not a bit like cold porridge, but that doesn't matter. It's the logical pattern of the brain that counts, not the grey stuff it's made of. The same with a computer. What matters is its logic. And the logic of a computer is really very simple. All it does is to read a list of instructions — we call this a program — and then it carries it out methodically. The only thing you have to do is to write down exactly what you want done in the language the computer understands. I know this may sound like a fanciful theory, but I assure you that it's not.

The computer at Manchester University has been working for over four years, since 1949, and it has successfully
tackled a wide variety of tasks. Many people think that
computers are glorified c-c-calculating machines. Not so.
It's true that computers are often used to do calculating
because they calculate very quickly — but computer prog-
rams don't have to have anything to do with numbers. A
colleague of mine has got our computer to hum tunes —
it once sang 'Jingle Bells'. We've even got it to write love
letters! Doing calculations, humming a tune, writing love
letters. These are very d-d-different tasks, but they're all
done by one machine — and that's an extremely important fact about computers. A computer is a universal
machine and I have *proved* how it can perform any task
that can be described in symbols. I would go further. It is
my view that a computer can perform any task that the
human brain can carry out. Any task. Now you might
think from what I've said that a computer can only do
what it's told to do. Well, it's true that we may start off
like that — but it's only the start. A computer can be
made to learn. Suppose, for example, that it were set to
play chess. It could find out for itself, in the light of its
own experience, which are winning and which are losing
strategies, and then drop the losing ones. After a while we
wouldn't know what instructions it was actually using. So
it would hardly be fair to say that we had instructed it
what to do. That would be like crediting the master with
any originality shown by the pupil. The question thus
arises as to whether or not we would credit such a
machine with intelligence. I would say that we must. What
I would very much like to do is to educate a computer,
partly by direct training and partly by letting it find out
things for itself. We don't know how to do this yet, but I
believe that it will be achieved in the near future. And I
feel sure that by the year 2000 it will be considered
perfectly correct to speak of an intelligent machine, or to
say that a computer is thinking. Of course, not everyone
agrees with this view; far from it. Some people say that
thinking is a function of man's immortal soul and since a
machine has no soul, it cannot think. Surely this is blas-
phemous. Who are we to deny the possibility that God
may wish to grant a soul to a machine? Then there is what
I call the 'Heads in the Sand' objection. 'The conse-

quences of machines thinking are too dreadful to contem-
plate,' people say. 'Such a thing could never happen.'
This point of view is usually expressed by intellectuals.
They have the most to lose. Another objection — this is
one I hear very frequently — is that a machine cannot be
said to think until it can write a sonnet or compose a
concerto, feel grief when its valves fuse, be warmed by
flattery, be angry or depressed when it can't get what it
wants. Well, of course, one might reply that there are
precious few human beings who can write a sonnet or
compose a concerto — and I can see no reason at all why
a thinking machine should not be kind, resourceful, and
beautiful, and friendly, have a sense of humour, tell right
from wrong, make mistakes, fall in love, or enjoy straw-
berries and cream. At the moment these considerations
should not concern us — but it might be rather nice,
don't you think, if, one day, we could find out what a
machine can feel?

[*Lighting change: autumn evening.*]

SCENE TWO

KNOX *enters, leaning heavily on a stick.*

KNOX: Did I tell you what happened to my brother?
TURING: What was that?
KNOX: They were having a dinner party. It was some time ago,
during the blitz. Eddie was just about to open a bottle of
claret when a bomb fell nearby. Tremendous explosion.
Bang! Guess what happened.
TURING: I've no idea.
KNOX: The blast was so severe that the cork shot straight out of
the bottle. Isn't that amazing? Eddie, of course, was quite
unperturbed. 'If only one could rely on its happening
regularly,' he said.
[KNOX *and* TURING *laugh; then* KNOX *frowns.*]
Why did I tell you that? There was something on my
mind. What was it? [*ponders*] Damn. My memory's hope-
less these days. I have to write everything down. [*smiles*]
Old age, that's the trouble. We all live far too long. My
solicitor says that dentists are to blame.

TURING: Yes, you told me.

KNOX: Did I? Ah. [*sits*] Have you been to London recently?

TURING: No, not for ages.

KNOX: The bomb damage is frightful. Rose Macaulay says that walking through St John's Wood is like walking through the ruins of Babylon. [*a sudden thought*] I know why I told you that story: dinner party — bottle of claret — [*opens a table drawer and takes out a bottle of whisky*] — real scotch! Would you like some?

TURING: Not for me, thank you.

KNOX: No . . . ?

TURING: Actually, I don't like it.

KNOX: Don't you? Neither do I. Isn't that a shame? Somebody gave it to me. Very nice of them. Ah, well — never mind. [*replaces the bottle*] I thought we should have a drink in honour of your trip to Washington.

TURING: I'm not going just yet.

KNOX: It's all settled, though?

TURING: So I believe.

KNOX: How do you feel about it?

TURING: Apprehensive. Wouldn't you? The Atlantic's a hazardous place — as we both know only too well. I have n-n-nightmares about an ocean full of U-boats.

KNOX: We'll all keep our fingers tightly crossed.

TURING: Please do. Actually, I'm rather intrigued. I'm intrigued to see what our American counterparts are like — whether code-breakers have national characteristics. Most probably they do, don't you think? Look at us. A b-b-benevolent patriarchy, ruled by the upper-middle-class. Independent, yet conformist. Cheerful in the face of adversity. And underneath it all, d-d-deeply ruthless.

KNOX: Ruthless?

TURING: Wouldn't you say?

KNOX: *Ruthless* . . . ?

TURING: Don't you remember how we cheered when we heard we'd captured an Enigma code-book? We only got it because a U-boat captain had been killed. Nobody thought about that. Not even me.

KNOX: I'd call that being realistic — not ruthless.

TURING: A b-b-bit of both, perhaps.

KNOX: Maybe. And maybe you're right about national characteristics. From what I know of the Americans — which isn't very much — they'll probably try to persuade you that their methods are far superior to ours.

TURING: They're worried — and who can blame them? It doesn't seem unreasonable to me that they should want to know how we're tackling the Enigma.

KNOX: I suppose not.

TURING: And they're not being ungenerous. As I understand it, they're prepared to tell us about their work on speech encipherment — and that could be tremendously important.

KNOX: You think so?

TURING: Oh yes. It's simply horrifying that all communications across the Atlantic have to go by short-wave radio. Anyone can listen.

KNOX: Even with speech scramblers?

TURING: They're easily penetrated. What's needed is an unbreakable speech encipherment system. But one doesn't exist. [*small smile*] Not yet anyway.

[KNOX *smiles. Brief pause. He looks at* TURING.]

KNOX: It's important that you're going.

TURING: It is.

KNOX: I mean it's important that it's you who are going and not some, uh . . . some more conventional representative.

TURING: Well, at least I know what I'm t-t-talking about.

KNOX: And you're going with Churchill's personal authority.

TURING: Yes.

KNOX: That's important, too. We're not very popular with the bureaucrats or the brass-hats. *Au contraire.* The fact that you're the one who's going to Washington is very significant.

TURING: I think that's mostly Churchill's doing.

KNOX: Oh, I'm sure of it. He knows how vital your work is: 'The geese who lay the golden eggs'; isn't that what he said?

TURING: He meant all of us.

KNOX: You in particular.

[TURING *glances at* KNOX.]

TURING: This is all very flattering, Knox. You're making me feel uneasy.

KNOX: Why is that?

TURING: I sense a sting in the t-t-tail approaching.

KNOX: Not a sting exactly. [*briefest pause*] I gather you've been chaining your tea mug to the radiator.

TURING: Not an unreasonable precaution. Tea mugs are in short supply

KNOX: Some people find it irritating.

TURING: I find it irritating that some people should be irritated.

KNOX: [*sighs*] I've come to the conclusion that the old cliché about eccentric artists is inaccurate. Scientists carry eccentricity to far greater lengths. [*a glance at silent* TURING] Not just you — others — your friend Wittgenstein, for example.

TURING: Wittgenstein is not a scientist.

KNOX: Philosopher, then; mathematician — does it matter? Even you must agree that he's dauntingly eccentric. And rude.
[*No response.*]
A friend of mine took me to meet him. There he was, this distinguished Fellow of Trinity, sitting in a deck-chair in a completely bare room. My friend introduced me and said that I would be interested in attending one of his classes. Wittgenstein looked at me with those cold, piercing eyes. 'My lectures are not for tourists,' he said.

TURING: [*a shrug*] He lives life as he chooses. What's wrong with that?
[*Brief pause.* KNOX *looks at* TURING.]

KNOX: I do think you ought to be a little more discreet.

TURING: About my tea mug?

KNOX: About this young engineer chap you've got working with you. Tongues are beginning to wag.
[TURING *stares at him.*]

TURING: Am I in for a lesson in morals?

KNOX: In common sense. I don't give a tuppenny damn whether you choose to go to bed with choirboys or cocker spaniels, but it would be wiser to keep your private life to yourself.

TURING: Is this an official reprimand?

KNOX: Friendly advice, nothing more. [*trying to adopt a more relaxed tone*] I mean, first things first; let's get our priorities right. What we're doing here — and most especially what you're doing here — has a direct and crucial bearing on the progress of the war. A pretty young engineer comes a rather poor second to that, surely?

TURING: Nobody complained when I was working with Pat.

KNOX: That was different.

TURING: Was it?

KNOX: Of course it was.

TURING: I thought you said rules only m-m-mattered in cricket.

KNOX: [*irritably*] Oh, it's such nonsense, this contemporary obsession with sexual fulfilment! Passion is dreadfully overrated, if you ask me. One is happiest when sex is a dimly remembered pleasure, like building sand-castles or climbing apple trees.

TURING: You can hardly expect me to agree with that.

KNOX: Like all of us, I can only speak from personal experience. I have been happily married for over twenty years, and I'm glad to say that passion has never played a significant rôle in our relationship. Understanding and companionship can be relied upon. Passion is forever fleeting.

TURING: Does that really matter?

KNOX: It matters to me.

TURING: Perhaps one brief moment of p-p-passion is worth more than twenty years of uneventful companionship.

KNOX: I didn't say it was uneventful. Anyway, we're not talking about me, we're talking about you.

TURING: I hear you're not very well.

[KNOX *stares.*]

KNOX: What's that got to do with it?

TURING: Nothing. I was changing the subject.

[KNOX *stares; says nothing.*]

Is it true? Are you ill?

KNOX: [*ignoring this*] Bear one thing in mind: a great many people — administrators and the military alike — regard Bletchley as a hot-bed of anarchy and unruliness. They pray for an excuse to bring us to heel.

TURING: [*furious*] The b-b-bureaucrats and the military should be bloody grateful to have me here!

KNOX: Most of them have spent their lives in a world of rigid discipline: rank, routine, procedure — that's all they know. Then you come along: work when you feel like it, complain about this, that and the other; ignore what few rules we do have here — and what's more, what's worse, you get away with it. You succeed. Can you blame them for disliking you?

TURING: They're small-minded. P-p-petty. Spiteful.

KNOX: Well, maybe.

TURING: What's the point of having a system that gives authority to people who d-d-don't deserve it? You say I complained — good God, of course I complained! — nothing was being done — you know that as well as I do — we needed more staff, m-m-more money, and absolutely bugger-all was

being done about it. If I hadn't written to Mr Churchill —
if I'd gone through the so-called proper channels — we'd
all be stuck here, twiddling our thumbs, with the Enigma
unbroken and most of our merchant ships on the b-b-
bottom of the Atlantic!

> [KNOX *tries to reply, but* TURING *is not to be si-
> lenced.*]

Do these people know how Churchill replied to my letter?
Do they? 'Make sure they have all they want on extreme
priority,' that's what he said.

KNOX: I know.

TURING: 'Action this day!'

KNOX: Yes, I know — and I'm not saying you did the wrong
thing: I'm just trying to explain why such, uh, unorthodox
methods are bound to cause a considerable upset.

TURING: All that m-m-matters is the work we do. Differences of
attitude, differences of personality, shouldn't come into it.

KNOX: They shouldn't, but they do.

TURING: Then they should be ignored.

KNOX: I think not.

TURING: Well, I do.

KNOX: You can't go through life ignoring the effect you have on
other people or the effect that other people have on you.

TURING: [*deliberately provocative*] You can try.

KNOX: You've spent far too much time thinking about your
Turing machines. We are, after all, human beings; and
you should try to accept the many imperfections that are
part of our human condition.

TURING: Tolerate, perhaps; not accept.

KNOX: Nevertheless, allowances have to be made; compromises
have to be reached.

TURING: I b-b-beg to differ.

KNOX: All right! — Let me give you an example. A few minutes
ago, you enquired about my health. Suppose I had
answered you directly. Suppose I had told you that I am
mortally ill and have only a year or so to live. Suppose I
had broken down and wept. Suppose I had opened my
heart to you and said that I had no wish to die; that I was
frightened and in despair. I can't believe that you would
have welcomed such a disclosure. I feel sure that you'd
have found it distressing, embarrassing and somewhat
inconsiderate. And so — being aware of your feelings as
well as my own — it would seem to be both correct and

appropriate for me to moderate my response.

[*Brief pause.* TURING *looks gravely at* KNOX.]

TURING: Are you dying?

KNOX: Similarly — or so it seems to me — when you reveal the nature of your sexuality, you cannot afford to ignore the effect it's bound to have on other people. Fear, for example; when people are asked to accept something they do not understand. Or anger — when what you so un-ashamedly reveal seems to be contrary to everything they've ever believed in. And pain. You're bound to cause a lot of pain. Not for yourself, necessarily — that's your concern, anyway — but for people who are close to you, anyone who's fond of you. Pain. Real pain.

[TURING *is silent; he looks at* KNOX. *Brief pause.*]

Speaking of Wittgenstein: he once wrote something that impressed me deeply. I sat down, there and then, with the book in my hand, and memorised what he had written. This is what he said: 'We feel that even when all possible scientific questions have been answered, the problems of life remain completely unanswered.'

[KNOX *exits.*]

[*Lighting change: crisp winter's day.*]

SCENE THREE

SARA *enters and goes to* TURING.

SARA: Alan, my dear, you are so silly!

[*She embraces him.*]

Why didn't you tell me you were coming down?

TURING: I wasn't sure I'd be able to make it. I didn't want to d-d-disappoint you.

SARA: Well, it's a wonderful surprise. I'm delighted.

[*Another embrace.*]

Just look at that dreadful jacket. I do wish you'd take more care of yourself. How long can you stay? Don't tell me you've got to go rushing back tomorrow morning.

TURING: I may have to.

SARA: Never mind, don't let's think about that. I've had the guest room completely redecorated. Such lovely curtains: Liberty print.

TURING: Mother, listen — I've got something to tell you.

[SARA *looks at him: a sudden intuition of bad news.*]

SARA: Something nice?

TURING: I'm afraid not.

[SARA *turns from him, not wishing to look at his face.*]

SARA: No, you wouldn't have come all this way to tell me anything nice. What is it?

TURING: Well, I . . . I'm in trouble.

SARA: What sort of trouble?

TURING: Serious trouble.

SARA: Tell me.

[TURING *opens his mouth to speak but cannot find the words.*]

TURING: It's so difficult to explain.

SARA: [*trying to help*] Is it something to do with your work?

TURING: [*shakes his head*] No.

[*Brief pause. He takes a step towards her.*]

Look — you know I've never been very interested in women.

SARA: People of your sort seldom are.

TURING: [*has she guessed the truth?*] M-m-my sort . . . ? What do you mean, my sort?

SARA: People who spend their lives with their heads buried in books.

TURING: It's nothing to do with that.

SARA: What, then?

TURING: I've no sexual feeling for women.

SARA: That's probably just as well. People seem to be getting divorced at such a rate these days.

TURING: Please listen. Please try to understand.

SARA: I'm doing my best.

TURING: The police have discovered that I'm having an affair with a boy.

[*Pause.* SARA *stares at him.*]

SARA: A boy . . . ? Do you mean a nancy boy?

TURING: Yes.

[*Pause.* SARA *stares; says nothing.*]

I'm sorry. There's no other way to t-t-tell you. I'm sorry.

[*Pause.*]

SARA: Will it be in the papers?

TURING: I don't know. Perhaps.

SARA: Have you told your brother?

TURING: Yes.

SARA: What did he say?

TURING: Shocked. Terribly shocked.

SARA: Thank God your father isn't alive. He was so proud of you.

> [*Pause.* TURING *remains silent.*]

Have you always . . . I mean — have you always been like this?

TURING: Yes.

SARA: Always?

TURING: Yes.

SARA: But what about that girl you were engaged to? What was her name? Pat.

TURING: I was never engaged to her.

SARA: I thought you loved her.

TURING: I was fond of her. I loved her as a friend.

> [*Pause*]

SARA: What's going to happen?

TURING: Well, uh . . . there'll be a t-t-trial.

SARA: They're sending you to court?

TURING: Yes.

SARA: When?

TURING: Soon. March. The end of March.

SARA: Will you go to prison?

TURING: P-p-possibly.

> [SARA *manages to control her distress. Pause.*]

SARA: How did the police find out? Did they catch you? Did they find you with this boy?

TURING: I told them.

SARA: Why? Why?

> [TURING *gives a hopeless shrug.*]

Oh, Alan.

TURING: I'm sorry.

> [SARA *gazes at him; she cannot prevent a surge of rage.*]

SARA: How could you bear to touch a man like that? How could you do such a thing?

> [*No response. Pause.* SARA*'s anger subsides.*]

Will it affect your career?

TURING: I suppose so.

SARA: How?

TURING: I don't know.

[*Pause. Then* SARA *goes to* TURING: *a decisive, direct movement.*]

SARA: What can I do to help?

TURING: [*amazed by this*] Well — nothing.

SARA: There must be something I can do. Let me. Please. You look so helpless.

TURING: That's how I feel.

[SARA *takes him by the hand.*]

SARA: Do you remember when you were at Hazelhurst? You must've been about ten or eleven. We'd all been up to Scotland for the summer holidays.

TURING: Lochinver.

SARA: Yes. Daddy went trout-fishing; I sketched. We had picnic teas in the heather. And then we had to go back to India, and you had to go back to school, back to Hazelhurst.

TURING: Yes.

SARA: Do you remember?

TURING: Of course I remember.

SARA: We took a taxi to the school and as we drove away you tried to run after us. You ran along the drive after the taxi. Your arms were flung wide; your mouth was open; you were saying something, shouting something, but I couldn't hear what it was. There were some shrubs by the school gates; rhododendrons, I think. It was like a great green curtain being pulled across in front of my eyes. The shrubs hid you from my sight. I couldn't see you any more. For a moment I felt quite breathless with panic. I wanted to jump out of the taxi, run back, and hold you in my arms for ever.

[*Pause.* TURING *embraces her.*]

TURING: I had no idea you felt like that.

[*They stand for a moment in still silence. Then* SARA *deliberately breaks the mood.*]

SARA: Do come and look at the guest room. I'm so pleased with it.

[TURING *and* SARA *exit.*]

[*Lighting change: February; rainy afternoon.*]

SCENE FOUR

ROSS *enters, carrying a file of papers; he sits at the table and quickly checks some documents.* TURING *approaches.*

ROSS: Mr Turing. Sit down. Make yourself comfortable.
> [TURING *sits.*]
You have to sign this first. Got a pen?

TURING: What is it?

ROSS: [*reading*] 'I, Alan Mathison Turing, have been told by Detective Sergeant Ross that I am not obliged to make any statement and that what I now say may be given in evidence. On that understanding I make the following statement.'

TURING: But you didn't tell me that. You didn't say I wasn't obliged to make a statement.

ROSS: Well, that's the standard perjury, sir.
> [TURING *decides not to pursue this any further.*]

TURING: Where do I sign?

ROSS: There, look — underneath what I've written.
> [TURING *signs.*]
That's it, fine.
> [*Brief pause.* TURING *appears to be waiting for instructions.*]
Right then, off you go.

TURING: What do you want me to say?

ROSS: Just describe how you met Ron Miller and what happened when he came to your house.
> [TURING *nods.*]
All right?

TURING: Yes. [*brief pause*] Um — do you want me to give dates and so on?

ROSS: If you can.

TURING: Well. Um. On December the 16th, 1951, I met Ron Miller in a public house near the Oxford Road station in Manchester. I invited him to come to my house on the following Friday evening.
> [*The rat-a-tat-tat of a front door knocker.* TURING *walks upstage and opens a door.* RON *enters.*]

RON: Sorry I'm late. Bloody buses. I waited damn near half an hour.
> [TURING *closes the door.*]

TURING: Take your coat off. I'll get you a drink.

RON: I bet you thought I wouldn't show up.

TURING: I thought you might've changed your mind.

RON: I said I'd be here, and here I am.

[TURING *smiles but says nothing.*]

Glad to see me?

TURING: Of course. Take your coat off.

[RON *does so; he looks around.*]

RON: Nice place. Been here long?

TURING: Just a few months. A year or so.

RON: Very nice. [*a grin*] Supper smells good.

TURING: [*brighter*] Ah well, I've prepared a sumptuous feast: home-made vegetable soup, roast leg of lamb, roast p-p-potatoes, carrots and Brussels sprouts. Apple crumble for pudding.

RON: All for a bloke you thought wouldn't show up.

TURING: I hoped.

[RON *smiles. Brief pause.*]

RON: What about that drink?

TURING: What would you like?

RON: Got a beer?

TURING: [*shakes his head*] Wine or Tizer.

RON: Tizer . . . ?

TURING: [*imitating an advertising jingle*] 'Tizer, Tizer, the appetizer.' [*smiles*] I'm testing it for its electrical conductivity.

RON: Why?

TURING: No reason. [*playfully*] It's what we call pure research.

RON: [*a frown*] What?

TURING: Nothing. A joke. [*grins*] Hungry?

RON: Starving!

[TURING *turns to address* ROSS.]

TURING: We had dinner. A bottle of wine. We talked about my work at the university, then I t-t-told him about *War and Peace*.

ROSS: About what?

TURING: The book by Tolstoy. Someone had lent it to me. I found it very impressive.

[TURING *resumes his scene with* RON.]

RON: I don't like war stories.

TURING: It's not really a war story; it's about two men. One is called Andrei, the other one is P-p-pierre. Andrei is ambitious and very energetic, but he's frightened of his own feelings. The other one, Pierre, is an extraordinary

man. He's awkward, ugly and rather shy, but he's full of
g-g-good-will and love. I like Pierre. He's a marvellous
character.

RON: I bet he gets killed.

[TURING *shakes his head.*]

TURING: Andrei gets killed. He gets shot at the Battle of Borodino.
It's a good book. You ought to read it.

RON: The battle of what?

TURING: Borodino.

RON: Never heard of it.

TURING: It's a place in Russia. A famous battle.

RON: I wasn't much good at history.

TURING: Now's your chance to learn. I'll help you.

[RON *is doubtful.*]

Let me get you a copy of the book. It's very good. Really.

RON: Okay.

TURING: Give it a try. Do read it.

RON: Yeah, okay. [*a grin*] How about another drink?

TURING: Help yourself. Sorry there's no beer. [*addresses* ROSS] I've
got an old violin at home. Ron thought it was great fun. I
p-p-played a couple of tunes on it, then Ron had a go,
then we talked some more about my work.

RON: How did it all start, then?

TURING: What?

RON: You being interested in science and things.

TURING: I've always been interested.

RON: Even as a kid?

TURING: Even then. [*glances at* RON; *smiles*] Yes, even then. [*brief
pause*] When I was a child, numbers were my friends.

RON: [*a frown*] Your what?

TURING: My friends. You know how it is; you know how children
have their own secret, make-believe friends; friends who
can always be trusted: dolls or teddybears or some old
piece of blanket they've k-k-kept and treasured since they
were babies. Comforters. Like familiar smells. My friends
were numbers. They were so wonderfully reliable; they
never broke their own rules. They were wonderfully se-
cure. They were safe. [*brief pause*] And then, when I was
about nine or ten, an uncle — uncle who? — uncle
somebody, I've forgotten who — this uncle g-g-gave me a
book for Christmas: *Natural Wonders Every Child Should
Know.* I thought it was the most exciting b-b-book I'd ever
read. It was, I suppose, looking back, a sort of gentle

introduction to the facts of life; there was a lot about chickens and eggs, I remember. [*smiles*] But what the writer of that book managed to convey was the idea that life — all life — is really a huge, all-embracing enterprise of science. There was no nonsense about God or d-d-divine creation. It was all science: chemicals, plants, animals, humans. 'The body is a machine,' he said. How exciting it was to read that! What an audacious, challenging, rather n-n-naughty, idea that was! He made life seem like a thrilling experiment. And I longed to take part in that experiment. [*pause; looks at* RON] Come here. Come and sit beside me.

        [RON *hesitates.*]

ROSS: And that's when the first offence occurred?

RON: Yes.

ROSS: Tell me what happened.

RON: After supper he told me about his work on the electronic brain. Then he started talking about some books he'd read. Then he asked me to sit next to him on the couch. Then he opened my trousers.

TURING: [*soliloquy*] 'Dear Mrs Morcom, I want to say how sorry I am about Christopher. I should be extremely grateful if you could find me sometime a little snap-shot of him. I shall miss his face so, and the way he used to smile at me sideways.'

RON: We listened to the wireless a bit and he played 'Cockles and Mussels' on his violin. I had a go on it. We went to bed about 11 o'clock. He put a towel on the bed sheet.

TURING: [*soliloquy*] In *War and Peace* there's a passage where Pierre meditates on his sense of shame. 'I must endure . . . what?' he asks. 'The disgrace to my name and to my honour? Oh, that's all rubbish!' he cries. 'Who is right, who is wrong? No one! While you are alive — *live*!'

RON: About 9 a.m. Turing got up and got dressed. He left his jacket on the arm of a chair and I knocked off eight pounds out of his jacket. We went into the parlour again. He leaned over me, put his head on my shoulder, and pulled my hand onto his legs; I wanked him again, but he never touched me.

TURING: [*soliloquy*] One thing is certain: a machine that is to imitate the brain must appear to behave as if it had free will. What does that mean?

RON: I didn't do this for my own benefit sexually, but I had

heard that you could get paid for it. I will never do it again
if I am given a chance. I know that it's wrong.

ROSS: Okay, Miller, wait outside.

[RON *exits.*]

TURING: [*soliloquy*] Tolstoy said that free will is merely an expression denoting what we do not know about the laws of
human life. Perhaps it's an illusion. But without that
illusion, life would be meaningless.

[ROSS *gathers together his papers and puts them into
the file.* TURING *remains motionless. Pause.* ROSS
looks at him.]

ROSS: What on earth made you do it?

TURING: Do what?

ROSS: Call the police. Talk about asking for trouble.

TURING: What else could I do?

ROSS: Sit still and keep quiet.

TURING: But I'd been robbed.

ROSS: Not exactly the crime of the century, was it?

[*No response.*]

All that rigmarole about a brush salesman . . . ! I've never
heard such rubbish in all my life. You must think I'm a
real prick.

TURING: I didn't want to involve Ron. I had to say something, and I
didn't want to involve Ron.

ROSS: We'd have found out sooner or later.

TURING: N-n-not necessarily.

ROSS: Of course we would. Questions get asked. Answers lead
to more questions. 'Why is a middle-aged, unmarried
professor spending the weekend with a bit of rough from
the Oxford Road?' Doesn't need a genius to work that one
out.

TURING: [*suddenly angry*] Look — I'd been robbed. I knew George
had robbed me. Why the hell should he get away with it?
If I had said nothing, it'd be like giving in to blackmail,
and I refuse to do that!

ROSS: Okay, fine, that's your decision. But you must've known
what would happen.

TURING: That didn't occur to me.

ROSS: [*eyebrows raised*] Didn't it, sir?

TURING: Not then. Not at the time. I didn't know you'd treat me
like a criminal.

ROSS: Not much choice, was there? When a man says he's
committed a crime I can't just ignore it.

TURING: G-g-going to bed with Ron is not a crime.

ROSS: It's against the law.

TURING: It's not as simple as that. Nothing ever is.

ROSS: In your opinion.

TURING: What's wrong with my opinion?

ROSS: Look, I don't care what you and young Ron get up to. But if it's against the law, I have to do something about it, okay?

TURING: Doesn't that worry you?

ROSS: Why should it?

TURING: Because the law makes everything black, white; right, wrong. Life's more complicated than that.

ROSS: You mean sex.

TURING: Not just sex.

ROSS: What, then?

TURING: All sorts of things. Mathematics. Even in mathematics there's no infallible rule for proving what is right and what is wrong. Each problem — each decision — requires fresh ideas, fresh thought. And if that's the case in m-m-mathematics — the most reliable body of knowledge that mankind has created — surely it might also apply in other, less certain, areas?

[ROSS *hesitates, thinking, before he replies.*]

ROSS: That's okay as a theory, sir, but it wouldn't work in real life.

TURING: Why not?

ROSS: Decisions have to be made; and if we can't decide what's right and what's wrong, then we've got to get someone — or something — to decide for us. All we've got is the law — and, in the present circumstances, that means me. [*picks up his file of papers*] Nothing personal, Mr Turing. I'm sorry this happened. I understand how you must feel.

TURING: No you don't. How can you?

[ROSS *looks at him. Brief pause.*]

ROSS: You're right, I don't. I can't. [*goes to a door*] You'll receive official notification of the committal proceedings. [*opening the door*] Keep it simple when you're in court, sir; all that stuff about mathematics wouldn't go down too well with the Wilmslow magistrates.

[ROSS *exits.*]

[*Lighting change: midday sun.*]

SCENE FIVE

PAT *enters, carrying picnic food on a tray.* TURING *spreads a raincoat on the ground.*

TURING: What did you get?

PAT: Spam sandwiches, fruit cake and lemonade.

TURING: Delicious.

PAT: There wasn't much of a choice, I'm afraid.

TURING: I should've taken you to a restaurant.

PAT: [*smiles*] This is fun.

> [*They start to eat.*]

It's good to see you, Prof.

TURING: It's good to see you.

PAT: Thank you for writing to me.

TURING: I wanted you to know what had happened. I wanted you to hear it from me, and not — well, second-hand.

PAT: Thank you.

TURING: It was in the *News of the World.* Northern edition. The headline said, 'Accused had Powerful Brain.' Could've been worse, I suppose — though that use of the past tense rather worried me.

> [PAT *smiles. They eat in silence for a moment.*]

PAT: I've thought about you a lot. It must've been awful.

TURING: Actually, not as bad as I feared. They put me in the cells during the trial. Being behind bars was by no means disagreeable. There was a wonderful absence of responsibility, rather like being back at school. [*referring to the sandwich*] Is that all right?

PAT: Fine. Did you think they'd send you to prison?

TURING: No, not really; I was a first offender, after all — first offender! — there's a laugh! I thought they'd most probably put me on probation. [*brief pause*] They're giving me drugs.

PAT: Who are?

TURING: They're giving me oestrogen, f-f-female sex hormones. It's supposed to kill male sexual interest. But it's only for a year; after that — everything returns to normal. We hope. [PAT *is shocked.*]

PAT: That's dreadful. Couldn't you refuse?

TURING: [*shakes his head*] I'm obliged to do it. I was placed on probation providing I agreed to the drug treatment. [*brief pause*] I'm growing breasts.

PAT: Oh, Alan.

TURING: Nobody seems to know whether or not they'll disappear when I stop taking the drugs. We'll have to wait and see.

PAT: God, how dreadful.

TURING: The embarrassment factor is high. I keep wondering whether I'll have to wear a b-b-bra.

[*He smiles.* PAT *remains silent; pause.*]

It was pretty awful going back to work after the trial. I didn't know how my colleagues would behave. I f-f-feared the worst. I was right. [*brief pause*] There was a predictable reaction from my brother.

PAT: Brother John.

TURING: Brother John, yes. Disgusted, repelled, incredulous, etcetera. He said I'd been a silly ass to g-g-go to the police. He was right.

PAT: What about your mother?

TURING: Yes, I dreaded telling her. I absolutely dreaded it. [*brief pause*] As it happens, she was wonderful about it. Quite remarkable. It seems to have drawn us c-c-closer together.

PAT: I'm glad.

TURING: Yes, so am I.

[*Pause.*]

PAT: What happened to the boy? The boy who, um . . .

TURING: Conditionally discharged. He's w-w-working in London, I think. I never see him. [*brief pause*] You're married?

PAT: Yes.

TURING: No job?

PAT: Just a housewife.

TURING: Are you happy?

PAT: Yes. Well, I suppose so. I don't think about it very much.

TURING: That means you are.

PAT: Does it?

TURING: You only think about being happy when you're not. Any children?

PAT: Two. Two boys.

TURING: I'd like to have had children. Is that a very sentimental thing to say?

PAT: Not in the least.

TURING: It sounds sentimental, coming from an old poof like me.

PAT: Don't say things like that.

TURING: It was supposed to be a joke.

[PAT *looks at him: concerned, tender.*]

PAT: I hope you're not too unhappy

TURING: I'm not unhappy at all. I enjoy my work; I have some good friends. I had a very jolly holiday. Norway.

PAT: [*surprised*] Norway . . . ?

TURING: No legal problems in Norway. And I met a charming young man called Kjell, who's promised to come and stay with me — all being well, all fingers crossed.

PAT: What sort of work are you doing?

TURING: I'm at Manchester University.

PAT: Yes, I know.

TURING: We've built a digital computer. You remember all my theorising about a universal machine? Well, we've done it, we've made one. — and it's all thanks to the work we did at Bletchley.

PAT: Why? How?

TURING: Electronics. Until we did it at B-b-bletchley, nobody had thought of using electronics to carry out logical operations — adding, multiplying and so on. And that's just what I needed — because to be of any p-p-practical use, a universal machine would have to carry out hundreds of thousands of logical operations every second. So electronics gave us the necessary speed — which left us with the problem of creating an adequate memory. If it's going to perform a reasonably significant task, a computer must keep a store of instructions and information in its m-m-memory — roughly the same as the contents of an average book. At first, we created a memory by using an acoustic delay line.

PAT: Using sound waves?

TURING: That's right. It takes a thousandth of a second for a sound wave to travel along a few feet of pipe — so the pipe could be regarded as storing the sound wave for that period.

PAT: The radar people used that idea during the war.

TURING: Yes — we pinched the idea and used a delay line to store the pulses of an electronic computer. But now, at Manchester, we're using little television screens — which means you can actually see the numbers and instructions stored in the machine. You can see them on the m-m-monitor tube: little bright spots.

PAT: How exciting. It must be very exciting.

TURING: Well, it would be if the organisation wasn't so rigid. Everything is strictly compartmentalised. You're either a mathematician or an engineer; you c-c-can't be both.

PAT: Unlike Bletchley.

TURING: Totally unlike Bletchley, more's the pity. But at least I'm able to use the computer for my own work. I've become increasingly interested in morphogenesis.

PAT: Embryology.

TURING: How do living things take shape? How do they know how to grow? I've got an idea which m-m-might explain how biological patterns arise — and I'm using the computer to simulate the growth patterns of p-p-plants and animals. But I'm still baffled by the Fibonacci patterns in a fir cone. Do you remember me telling you about that?

PAT: Yes.

TURING: One summer afternoon, when you thought you were in love with me.

PAT: I went to church with your mother and cried all through the sermon.

> [TURING *looks at her; he reaches out, gently touching her hand.*]

You haven't changed at all.

PAT: [*smiles*] It's nice of you to say so.

TURING: It's true. [*brief pause*] It seems an awfully long time since we were at Bletchley.

PAT: Doesn't it?

TURING: A lifetime. [*brief pause*] I never found that silver.

PAT: What silver?

TURING: Those silver ingots I buried.

PAT: [*smiles*] Oh yes.

TURING: I searched high and low. Never found them.

PAT: [*smiles*] I wonder if your tea mug is still chained to the radiator.

TURING: [*smiles*] Yes, I got ticked off about that.

PAT: Who by?

TURING: Dillwyn Knox.

PAT: Poor Mr Knox. [*brief pause*] I went to see him when he was ill . . . near the end.

TURING: That was good of you.

PAT: I was fond of him. He had a house in the Chilterns. Surrounded by trees. Terribly damp. Mr Knox kept apologising for the draughts. 'The only places where you can feel reasonably warm are my study and the airing cupboard,' he said.

> [TURING *laughs. Pause.*]

I suppose you heard about his romance with Maynard Keynes?

TURING: [*incredulous*] What?

PAT: Didn't you know?

TURING: Knox . . . ?

PAT: When he was young.

TURING: Are you sure?

PAT: An uncle of mine was at school with him.

TURING: Good God.

PAT: Lytton Strachey, too — but that was at Cambridge, not Eton.

TURING: [*amazed*] He was Lytton Strachey's lover . . . !

PAT: Apparently.

TURING: Well, he never told me. He never even dropped a hint.

PAT: I thought perhaps you knew.

TURING: I hadn't the remotest idea.

PAT: I don't think anybody paid much attention to it. Everything's so very different when you're at school or at Cambridge.

TURING: Good God Almighty.

PAT: It was all a thing of the past; he was devoted to his wife.

TURING: Yes, he told me. [*glancing at* PAT] That's the thing to do, of course: have your f-f-fling when you're young and conform later. [*smiles*] I should've married you. All this would never have happened. I should've p-p-played the game and stuck to the rules.

PAT: Why didn't you?

TURING: I couldn't.

PAT: [*gently mocking him*] Silly ass.

TURING: [*smiles*] Yes.

[*Brief pause;* PAT *stands up.*]

PAT: Would you like an ice cream?

TURING: I'll get it.

PAT: My treat. Wafer or cornet?

TURING: Er — wafer.

[PAT *exits.*]

[*Lighting change: late afternoon; darkening skies.*]

SCENE SIX

JOHN SMITH *enters: the authoritative man last seen in Act One, Scene Four.*

TURING *rises to his feet.*

SMITH: Mr Turing? I'm sorry to keep you waiting. Everything's at sixes and sevens here today.
[*He shakes hands with* TURING.]
My secretary's gone down with 'flu, and the temporary girl doesn't seem to know that she's doing. Do sit down, won't you? [*gestures to a chair*] It's good of you to come along at such short notice. Thank you very much.
[TURING *sits.*]

TURING: Your letter was rather vague.

SMITH: Was it?

TURING: Official, but rather vague.

SMITH: Well, it's just one of those things that are done better by a meeting than by telephone. Basically, it's a question of keeping in touch.

TURING: What do you mean?

SMITH: You're a brilliant man, Mr Turing — unique, in many ways — and there's no point in trying to deny it.

TURING: I wasn't going to.

SMITH: This country has always tended to take its brilliant men for granted. That's a mistake. A serious mistake. We can't afford to make mistakes like that.

TURING: Who are you? I've no idea who you are.

SMITH: Sorry, sorry, sorry. My name is Smith, John Smith. [*smiles*] Nobody believes it. I have a dreadful time with hotel clerks. Anyway, the point is this: it would be foolish to pretend that your homosexuality hasn't created certain problems, certain anxieties.

TURING: [*bristling*] For whom?

SMITH: [*ignoring this*] But providing we can discuss the situation reasonably, I feel sure that these anxieties can be reduced to a minimum.

TURING: What anxieties?

SMITH: As I say, it's just a question of keeping in touch.

TURING: You're talking about security p-p-problems.

SMITH: I am. Of course I know you haven't been involved with intelligence work since your, uh, difficulty with the law; nevertheless, the knowledge remains, does it not?

TURING: [*angry*] You don't trust me.

SMITH: We have to be careful. Increasingly careful. And it's not just us. The Americans are getting jumpy. They've given you access to some very sensitive information — for instance, the speech encipherment material. An unguarded word could so easily fall into the wrong ears.

> [TURING *looks at him; says nothing.*]

There is a general feeling of unease.

TURING: About me?

SMITH: We know that you are a man of the greatest integrity. Your essential loyalty has never been questioned.

TURING: [*voicing the unspoken word*] But.

SMITH: All possibilities have to be considered.

TURING: Such as?

SMITH: Can you, in all honesty, say that you would never — never, under any circumstances — reveal something of your work to a sexual partner?

> [TURING *opens his mouth to make an immediate response, but then hesitates for a moment.*]

TURING: No, of course not.

SMITH: No, you would — or no, you wouldn't?

TURING: No, I can't say — in all honesty — that such a circumstance would n-n-never arise. Neither can you. Who could?

SMITH: [*smoothly avoiding a direct response*] That being the case, one's attention is drawn to the choice of partner. [*briefest pause*] It seems that you have an unusually wide range of acquaintances.

> [TURING *smiles mirthlessly.*]

TURING: You mean it would be all right if I went to bed with other m-m-mathematicians? Preferably from one of the older universities. Preferably from one of the more distinguished p-p-public schools. Preferably with what the Americans call Security Clearance.

SMITH: [*drily*] I'm sure that would make us all a lot happier. [*a glance at* TURING] Sorry, that was rather glib. But you must realise that your work for the intelligence service means that you are simply not free to behave as you might choose. You have had extremely unusual access to secret information; this carries with it a heavy — and sometimes irksome — responsibility.

TURING: [*angered by* SMITH's *patronising tone*] I am aware of that.

SMITH: [*chastened*] Yes, I'm sure you are. [*brief pause*] It may seem like interference; in fact, we're trying to be helpful.

TURING: Oh? How?

SMITH: By preventing any further errors of judgement.

TURING: Meaning what exactly?

SMITH: This young Norwegian — Kjell.

> [TURING *is amazed.*]

I think it would be unwise for him to visit you here.

TURING: How do you know about Kjell?

SMITH: Somebody told me.

TURING: Who?

SMITH: I forget.

> [TURING *is sceptical.*]

Truly.

TURING: Am I being watched?

SMITH: You're a valuable man. You have valuable information stored away inside that — what did you call it? — inside that bowl of cold porridge. [*small smile*] I have a nephew at Sherborne. He was most impressed by your lecture. [*brief pause*] We have to make sure that this knowledge is properly protected.

> [TURING *is silent, apparently considering the situation.* SMITH *looks at him.*]

I can guess what's going through your mind.

TURING: Can you?

SMITH: You're feeling outraged; outraged and resentful.

TURING: As a matter of fact, I was thinking about the Duke of Windsor. I was appalled by the way he was bounced into exile. Most particularly, I was appalled by the hypocrisy of the Establishment: Mrs Simpson was okay as his m-m-mistress, but as his wife — never! I felt it was shameful of the State to interfere with a man's private life; and I was convinced that the government wanted to get rid of him and used Mrs Simpson m-m-merely as an excuse. [*brief pause*] But then, later, I heard that he'd been extremely lax about state d-d-documents, leaving them about and letting Mrs Simpson and friends see them. I changed my mind about the Abdication. A man who does that shouldn't be King. [*pause; looks at* SMITH] When you say 'keeping in touch', what precisely do you mean?

SMITH: We'd like to be told about any change of residence, any change in your working life, any trips abroad, that sort of thing.

[TURING *nods.*]

Are you planning to go abroad this year?

TURING: Yes, I'm going to Greece.

SMITH: When?

TURING: May.

SMITH: Whereabouts in Greece?

TURING: Corfu.

SMITH: Oh, it's very nice there, you'll like it a lot; and May is the perfect time to go.

[TURING *and* SMITH *stand facing each other. Pause.*]

TURING: I want you to know that I have no regrets about m-m-my involvement with the intelligence service. The work I did at Bletchley was very important to me.

SMITH: Yes, I'm sure.

TURING: Important in a way that you probably c-c-cannot understand. [*brief pause*] Everything came together there. All the strands of my life. My work as a mathematician. My interest in ciphers. My ability to solve practical problems. My love of my country. [*brief pause*] For a year or so, I felt I had found what I had b-b-been searching for.

[*Pause.* SMITH *exits.*]

[*Lighting change: bars of sunshine through shuttered windows.*]

SCENE SEVEN

NIKOS, *a Greek boy of about 20, lies face down on the divan; asleep; naked, apart from a towel wrapped around his waist. An abandoned sheet lies on the floor; nearby, on a table, is a large, old-fashioned radio.*

TURING *goes to the divan and looks down at* NIKOS.

TURING: Are you really asleep or are you just pretending?

[*No response.*]

Not that it matters much. I suppose. [*looks at* NIKOS; *smiles*] Nikos from Ipsos. Never before have I been to bed with someone I couldn't talk to. The Greek phrasebook doesn't cover these circumstances, alas. [*yawns; looks at his wristwatch*] Half-past five. That means it's — what? — half-past three at home. They'll soon be having tea in the laboratory. Tea and buns. Outside it'll be grey — overcast — drizzle. The start of another grey, chilly evening in Manchester. [*wanders across the room; sees the radio*] My God. Look at that wireless! A real museum piece. [*switches on the radio; nothing happens*] Doesn't work. Ah well, never mind. [*mock north country accent*] Mustn't expect too much in this life. [*looks at* NIKOS; *smiles*] Nikos from Ipsos. Perhaps I should take you back to Manchester with me. You might like it. You might even f-f-find it rather exciting. [*dismisses the fantasy*] No — you'd end up a waiter. Fat and paunchy. Married to a cashier from Boots. [*returns to the radio*] I wonder why this thing doesn't work?

> [TURING *examines the radio and removes the back panel; he peers at the valves and wires.* NIKOS *stirs; he looks at* TURING.]

NIKOS: Den doulevi.
> [*It doesn't work.*]
> [TURING *turns to* NIKOS.]

TURING: This doesn't work.

NIKOS: Den doulevi.

TURING: Your wireless doesn't work.

NIKOS: Ine spasmeno.
> [*It's broken.*]

TURING: Is that what you're telling me? Are you saying this thing doesn't work.

NIKOS: Ine spasmeno.

TURING: I'll mend it for you, shall I? Would you like me to do that? [*tries to mime mending the radio*] Shall I try to mend it?
> [NIKOS *stares at him.*]

NIKOS: Den katalaveno.
> [*I don't understand.*]

TURING: Perhaps I can mend it. Would you like me to try? I'm rather g-g-good at that sort of thing. [*more mime*] Mend it. Me — mend — wireless — okay?

NIKOS: Borite na to diorthosete?
> [*You can mend it?*]

TURING: I'll need a screwdriver. [*more mime*] To loosen the screws. Do you have a screwdriver?
> [NIKOS *understands: a beaming smile.*]

NIKOS: Hriazeste ena katsavidi! Tha sas vro ena. . .

> [*You need a screwdriver! I'll find you one . . .*]
>> [NIKOS *exits;* TURING *returns to the radio.*]

TURING: Let's have a look at this thing. I've always taken a p-p-
particular pride in my practical skills. What's the point of
being a theorist if you can't put your theories into prac-
tice?

> [NIKOS *enters, holding a screwdriver.*]

NIKOS: Katsavidi.

> [*Screwdriver.*]

TURING: Oh good, you've found one.

NIKOS: Katsavidi.

TURING: [*taking the screwdriver*] Thank you.

NIKOS: [*emphatically*] Katsavidi.

TURING: Oh — that's the word, is it?

NIKOS: Katsavidi!

TURING: Katsavidi.

NIKOS: [*grinning*] Ne — katsavidi!

TURING: Katsavidi. Well, that's wonderful, thank you very much. If
I ever need to buy a screwdriver in Greece, I'll know what
to ask for, won't I? [*starts unscrewing valves and wires*] Ah, I
see what's wrong with it. [*smiling at* NIKOS] Nikos from
Ipsos. Talking to you is like talking to a psychoanalyst.
The same absence of response. The same unanswered
question: I wonder what he's thinking? [*another smile*]
Actually it's quite relaxing. Rather comforting. [*re-wires
the faulty section*] I went to an analyst for a time. About a
couple of years ago. There'd been some t-t-trouble with
the police. I was prosecuted for an offence the British
quaintly call Gross Indecency. I was prosecuted and sent
for trial. It was a very disturbing and unpleasant experience. That's why I went to the analyst. I told him everything. Almost. Even my dreams. And he'd just sit there
and listen to me. He'd sit there and listen and listen and
listen. Just like you. Nikos from Ipsos. The idea was to
integrate thinking and feeling. That's what Jungian analy-
sis is all about. The integration of thinking and feeling. A
tall order, in my case. [*replaces the back panel of the radio*]
Right. Good. [*turning to* NIKOS] You can try it now. Try it.

NIKOS: Ti . . . ?

> [*What . . . ?*]

TURING: Switch it on.

NIKOS: Ine etimo? To diorthosete?

> [*Is it ready? Have you mended it?*]

TURING: It should work now. [*mimes*] Switch it on.

                    [NIKOS *steps forward cautiously; he switches on the radio: a loud burst of Greek dance music.* NIKOS *shouts with delight and embraces* TURING.]

NIKOS: To diorthosete! To kanate na doulevi!
      [*You've mended it! You've made it work!*]

TURING: Thank you, thank you — that's enough.

             [TURING *disentangles himself from* NIKOS*'s embrace and switches off the radio.*]

NIKOS: Iste poli exypnos — poli exypnos anthropos. Afto to radio den doulepse yia pollous mines. To pira sena filo pou xeri apo radia, ke ipe ine para poli palio, ke pote den tha xanadoulepsi. Ma ine kalo radio — to xero — ke yiafto to filaxa. Den borousa na to petaxo. Ka tora to kanate na doulevi. Iste poli exypnos anthropos!
      [*You are very clever — a very clever man. That radio hasn't worked for many months. I took it to a friend who knows about radios, and he said it was too old, it would never work again. But it's a good radio — I know that — and so I kept it. I couldn't bear to throw it away. And now you have fixed it. You have made it work. You are a very clever man!*]

TURING: Well, I've no idea what that was all about — but I'm glad you're so pleased.

NIKOS: Iste poli exypnos anthropos!
      [*You are a very clever man!*]

             [NIKOS *kisses* TURING, *who is both touched and embarrassed.*]

TURING: Thank you, Nikos dear. Thank you. [*smiles*] It's a good feeling, isn't it? Solving a problem, finding the answer. Making it work. A good feeling. It's all like that wireless, really, It's all a question of making the right connections. [*brief pause; an idea slips into his mind*] Shall I tell you a secret? Top secret. I couldn't even tell my analyst about this. But since you won't understand a single word, it doesn't really matter. It all took place at the beginning of the war in a country house called Bletchley Park. The Germans had built a machine called the Enigma. It was very cunning. It made codes — and the Germans believed it was completely foolproof: unbreakable. But somehow we had to break it. If we didn't, if we couldn't, we'd lose the war — it was as simple as that. The machine itself didn't look very complicated: rather like a typewriter. A few had been captured, you see, so we knew how it worked. There was a typewriter keyboard — and behind the keyboard, three rotors. The letters of the alphabet were on each rotor. When you pressed a letter on the keyboard, electricity flowed along a wire to the rotors and out again. As a result, one letter was encoded into another: an A, for example, would be encoded into an M. At the same time, the rotors turned — so that if you pressed A again, it would be encoded into a different letter — a W, perhaps, a P, an S, or whatever. The jumbled-up message would be decoded by an operator with another Enigma machine. He'd also know the starting point of the rotor positions — which were changed every day. This was central to the whole system; everything rested on those rotor positions — which were transmitted separately and secretly, and which we had no means of guessing. The three rotors created 26 times 26 times 26 permutations: 17,576. With a degree of patience, it was possible — *possible* — to find the right rotor position. But what made the system virtually unbreakable was the fact that the Germans had attached a plugboard to the Enigma machine. It was like a telephone switchboard. You just connected pairs of letters with jackplugs — an A with an M, say — and this swapped the letters before they were fed into the rotors. This resulted in thousands of millions of possible permutations, and this was the problem we had to solve. Where to begin? Well, first, there was guesswork. The code-breaking process always began with a guess. We had to guess what the first few words of the message were. This wasn't as difficult as it sounds because military messages invariably start with a stereotyped phrase: the date, the time, the name and rank of the sender, that sort of thing. We were lucky at Bletchley — we had a wonderfully good guesser. Dillie Knox. His guesses were almost always right. Then we discovered that it was possible to use the few words we'd guessed to form a chain of implications, of logical deductions, for each of the rotor positions. If this chain of implications led you to a contradiction — which was usually the case — it means you're wrong, and you have to move onto the next position. And so on and so on and so on. An impossibly lengthy and laborious process — but, in essence, a *mechanical* one! And so — we designed and built an entirely new sort of machine to do the job for us.

Inside: rotors, like the Enigma. The rotors would spin round, trying several possible positions every second. At each position, electricity flowed — stopping only when a consistent rotor and plugboard position was reached. The trouble was, it was still too slow — far too slow. Speed was essential, and our machines would take days — sometimes weeks — to reach a solution. And then, one afternoon, I remembered a conversation I'd had with Wittgenstein some months before; we were arguing about the fact that a contradiction implies any proposition. Wittgenstein said that this was just a useless language-game — but on the spring afternoon at Bletchley, I saw — immediately — how this idea could have a practical application to our code-breaking machine. If your guess is wrong, then the electricity would flow through all the other hypotheses and knock them out in a flash — like the chain reaction in an atomic bomb. If your guess is correct, everything would be consistent — and the electrical current wouldn't flow past the correct combination. By using this idea, our machine could examine thousands of millions of permutations at amazing speed — and could thus reach a solution in hours rather than days. We had found the 'way in'. More than that: all the connections had been made. There was the pure beauty of the logical pattern. The human element. The deeply satisfying relationship between the theoretical and the practical. What a moment that was. Quite, quite extraordinary. It was a wonderfully sunny day, I remember. The lawn had just been cut, and everywhere there was the smell of freshly mown grass. I could hear a wireless playing in one of the huts: dance music — a silly tune that was very popular in those days. [*sings*] 'It's a hap-hap-happy day

> Toodle, oodle, oodle, oodle, ay.
> For you and me,
> For us and we,
> All the clouds have roll'd away.'
> [*Pause.*]

In the long run, all things considered, it's not breaking the code that matters — it's where you go from there. That's the real problem. [*pause*] Oh, Christopher . . . If only you could've been there. Never again. Never again a moment like that.

SCENE EIGHT

The telephone rings. ROSS *hurries to the telephone; he is carrying a cardboard box and several files. He puts the box and the files on the table and grabs the telephone receiver.*

ROSS: Hello, Ross . . . Okay, fine. [*hangs up and goes to the door*] Come in, Mrs Turing.

[SARA *enters.*]

Do sit down. Can I get you a cup of tea or something? A cup of coffee?

[SARA *sits.*]

SARA: No, thank you.

ROSS: Right, um —[*indicating the cardboard box*] — these are your son's belongings. As you know, a few odds and ends had to be examined before the coroner could complete his report. Here's a list; you'd better make sure everything's there.

SARA: Do I have to?

ROSS: Not if it upsets you.

SARA: I think I'd rather not.

[ROSS *takes an envelope from his jacket pocket and gives it to* SARA.]

ROSS: I kept this separately. It's his medal, his O.B.E. I was afraid it might get lost.

SARA: [*puts it into her handbag*] Thank you.

[ROSS *gives her a document.*]

ROSS: If you'll just sign here, please.

[SARA *signs.*]

Good, thank you. [*takes the document*] I didn't know he'd got the O.B.E. He never told me. What was it for?

SARA: The work he did during the war. Whatever that was. [*sighs*] There are so many things I know nothing about; so many things I don't understand.

ROSS: Yes, it's a sad business. I'm very sorry.

SARA: Of course, it was all a dreadful mistake.

ROSS: In what way?

SARA: The coroner's verdict.

ROSS: [*non-committal*] Ah, well . . .

SARA: To say that my son took his own life is quite ridiculous. It was obviously a tragic accident. The coroner's verdict is a disgrace.

ROSS: I can't really offer an opinion, Mrs Turing.

SARA: You met him. Do you think he was the sort of man to commit suicide?

ROSS: It's two or three years since I've seen him, and you never know what people might do in extreme circumstances.

SARA: Let me tell you something about my son. His first day at Sherborne was also the first day of the General Strike. He bicycled all the way from Southampton to Sherborne — sixty miles! — so that he would be sure of getting to school on time. It was reported in the local newspaper. A boy who could do that would never take his own life.

[ROSS *looks at her; says nothing.*]

He had everything to live for. Everything.

SCENE NINE

TURING *is sitting downstage in a pool of grey Manchester light.*

Pause.

TURING: Mr Headmaster, members of the staff, boys . . . [*pause*] What is needed is the ability to take ideas seriously and to follow them through to their logical if upsetting conclusion. Thus. Can the mind exist without the body? Can mental processes take place in something other than a living brain? [*pause*] How are we to answer that question satisfactorily? Is it possible to do so? Or is it simply unprovable? An eternal Entscheidungsproblem? Forever undecidable . . . ? [*pause; then almost vivaciously*] Being a practical man as well as a theorist, I tend to look for practical solutions; in this case namely, viz., to dispose of the body and to release what is left. A mind. Or a nothing. [*goes to one of the tables and opens a drawer; takes out an apple and a small tin*] Here I have an ordinary apple: red and ripe and English. And here — a tin containing potassium cyanide. [*the ghost of a smile*] Nothing could be easier, could it? [*dips the apple into the potassium cyanide and raises the fruit to his lips*] Dip the apple in the brew, let the sleeping death seep through.

THE END